11+ Vocabulary: 1400 words testing Synonyms/ Antonyms/ Homophones/ Homographs/ Idioms/ Cloze

In 10 minute Verbal Reasoning tests

By

Jerome K

Copyright Notice

All rights reserved.

Do not duplicate or redistribute in any form.

How to use this book

This book tests over 1400 words that frequently appear in the 11 plus exam, both CEM as well as GL and Independent schools exams.

There are 42 sets containing 34 questions each.

Each set should be done in 10 minutes.

Try to set aside a period of 30-60 minutes each day and do one or two tests.

Short periods of regular study are more effective than long irregular sessions.

Make a note of the questions you get wrong, and revise them with the help of the answers and Explanations given at the end of this book.

To learn new words;

- Study the definition, part of speech and example sentences with the help of a dictionary.
- Practice saying the word aloud.
- Some students find it helps to copy out the words in a notebook to learn the spelling.
- If you have a study partner try to explain to him/her what the word means.
- Try to write your own example sentence using the new word.

Tips for taking the tests

- Since the tests are timed, you should <u>not</u> spend too much time on any one question.

- Ensure that you read the instructions carefully, e.g. sometimes students may confuse an antonym question for a synonym one, and select incorrect answers for the whole section!

- <u>After the test</u>, make sure that you learn ALL the words in the tests, and not just the ones that a question may be asking specifically.
  e.g. If you are asked to find the <u>synonym</u> for **deft,** and you may already know that the correct answer is **adept**, but ensure that you also learn the meanings of <u>all</u> the other answer choices while revising the test. (*bungling, maladroit, amateur and feeble*).
  The words used are the ones that commonly appear in the 11 plus tests so being familiar with more of them will result in a higher score.

- For the *'Fill in blanks type'* questions, you may need to skip a question if you get stuck, but come back to it after reading more of the text. This will provide further context/clues that may enable you to now answer the question.

- At the end of each test, blank space is provided for you to write down the words you do not know, enabling easier revision.

Set 1

A. Synonyms

Select the word that most closely matches the meaning of the word provided.

1.	**pandemonium**	quiet	turmoil	orderly	organised	logical
2.	**feckless**	irresponsible	efficient	supportive	purposeful	effective
3.	**aplomb**	gaucheness	misgiving	fear	anxiety	imperturbability
4.	**deft**	bungling	maladroit	adept	amateur	feeble
5.	**egregious**	slight	flagrant	shabby	insignificant	piddling
6.	**jargon**	shrewd	profound	formal	vernacular	standard
7.	**meander**	wander	determine	conclude	bolt	gush
8.	**precipice**	plateau	slope	trough	prairie	cliff

B. Fill in the blanks

Fill in the blanks from the words in the table below. There are two extra words you do not need.

torrential	locate	injured	reported	strike	smashed	evacuate

1. Typhoon Jongdari is the latest storm to _____ Western and Central Japan. Winds in excess

2. of 100mph and _____ rain made landfall in Mie Prefecture, Honshu. Tens of

3. thousands of people were ordered to _____ ahead of the storm. It has been

4. reported that dozens of people have been _____, but no deaths or missing persons

5. have been reported. In one incident the rough sea _____ through the window of a

   hotel restaurant in Atami, injuring five people.

C. Antonyms

Pick the word that means the opposite or near opposite of the word provided.

1.	**cantankerous**	crotchety	irritable	pleasant	peevish	cranky
2.	**gallant**	manful	cowardly	gutsy	courageous	proud
3.	**intricate**	simple	complicated	detailed	complex	fancy
4.	**jocular**	facetious	solemn	jocund	witty	jovial
5.	**taboo**	banned	improper	acceptable	forbidden	discouraged
6.	**noxious**	unhealthy	fatal	salubrious	poisonous	toxic
7.	**sombre**	cheerful	dismal	melancholy	dreary	doleful
8.	**banal**	trite	stale	extraordinary	insipid	humdrum

D. Missing letters

Fill in the missing letters to complete the words in the boxes below.

1. The coconut is one of the most | u | | e | f | | | trees in existence.

2. The milk of the young coconut is a | n | | | r | | t | | | u | s |

3. drink. A sweet | l | i | | | i | | obtained from the buds, ferments readily

4. and is used as a | | e | v | | | a | | e | both when fresh and

5. distilled. It may also be boiled to make | v | | r | i | | u | s | palm sugars.

E. Homophones and homographs

Homophones are two or more words having the same pronunciation but different spellings and meanings. Homographs are words which have the same spelling but different meanings.

From the list below, fill in the blanks. (The first one has been done for you).

master	race	address	maze	maize

1. The location where you live — _____address_____
2. A place that is hard to find the way out of — _____
3. An expert in a particular skill e.g. painting — _____
4. To speak or write to someone or to direct attention to a problem — _____
5. Memorise or practice something — _____
6. A group of persons who come from the same ancestor — _____
7. A competition to be the first to do something — _____
8. A cereal crop widely grown in many parts of the world — _____

Set 2

A. Synonyms

Select the word that most closely matches the meaning of the word provided.

1. **listless**   enthusiastic   (languid)   active   alert   keen
2. **nadir**   zenith   climax   summit   (bottom) acme
3. **feral**   (ferocious)   tame   domestic controlled civilized
4. **arcane**   common   clear   (obscure) known   normal
5. **fractious**   obedient   patient   amicable complaisant (petulant)
6. **instigate**   (bring about)   calm   pacify   appease   subdue
7. **decry**   laud   (denounce)   appreciate commend exalt

B. Fill in the blanks

Fill in the blanks from the words in the table below. There are two extra words you do not need.

queue	herbivorous	interesting	ecstatic	nauseous	extinct	expensive

1. I enjoy going to the Ocean Park. Most of the sights there are _____. There were a lot

2. of people waiting for the Penguin Dance so we had to _____ up. After watching the

3. Penguin Dance, we decided to try the Sky Jump. I felt _____ after trying it as we were

    tossed in the air several times. The next attraction we tried was the Dino Park. One of the

4. guides pointed out the Ankylosaurus, which was a _____ dinosaur, which

5. only ate plants. He also said that the dinosaurs became _____ due to an asteroid impact

    millions of years ago.

C. Antonyms

Pick the word that means the opposite or near opposite of the word provided.

1.	**admissible**	allowable	acceptable	tolerable	forbidden	permitted
2.	**ballistic**	angry	pleased	raving	rabid	wrathful
3.	**obtrude**	keep out	interfere	meddle	poke	intrude
4.	**yelp**	howl	scream	whisper	squeal	yell
5.	**eccentric**	bizarre	erratic	weird	common	quirky
6.	**extol**	glorify	abase	laud	acclaim	compliment
7.	**alacrity**	haste	willingness	eagerness	reluctance	dispatch

D. Missing words

Choose the best word to complete the sentences.

The majority of the people during the Middle ages worked as farmers. They planted

(1) _____ (fruits, crops, vegetables) such as barley, wheat, peas and oats. They also

(2) _____ (taken, took, take) care of animals such as chickens and cows to provide them

with eggs and milk, (3) _____ (subsequently, vigorously, respectively). During the Middle

Ages, there were lords who owned large areas of land. They lived in large houses called a

(4) _____ (bungalow, manor, lighthouse) or a castle. All the wealthy people

(5) _____ (wore, worn, dressed) nice clothes made of wool, velvet or silk, while the peasants

wore plain clothing made of heavy wool.

E. Odd one out

Four of the words in each list are linked. Mark the word that is not related to these four.

Example: red   green   ~~stripy~~   blue   yellow

1.	guitar	flute	violin	harp	cello
2.	boat	yacht	ferry	submarine	airplane
3.	giggle	cackle	cry	laugh	snicker
4.	eyes	retina	iris	tongue	pupil
5.	division	addition	subtraction	equation	multiplication

F. Idioms

Match each idiom to its meaning.

1. **Add fuel to the fire**   a. Behave properly
2. **Get your act together**   b. To add another problem to an existing problem
3. **To be in the same boat**   c. I forgot something
4. **To cold shoulder someone**   d. To ignore someone
5. **It slipped my mind**   e. To be in the same difficult situation as someone else

Set 3

A. Synonyms

Select the word that most closely matches the meaning of the word provided.

1.	**chide**	compliment	approve	emulate	rebuke	appreciate
2.	**abstruse**	recondite	comprehensible	concrete	lucid	direct
3.	**jittery**	nervous	easy	calm	unshakable	relaxed
4.	**liaison**	disconnection	alienation	cooperation	disintegration	remoteness
5.	**poignant**	unimpressive	emotional	restless	insipid	bland
6.	**avarice**	greed	philanthropy	benefaction	liberality	compassion
7.	**mitigated**	aggravated	relieved	intensified	incited	agitated
8.	**obliterate**	preserve	protect	save	conserve	eradicate

B. Fill in the blanks

Fill in the blanks from the words in the table below. There are two extra words you do not need.

| dominant | twice | lost | clinched | sweep | rivalry | crucial |

1. The Golden State Warriors _____ their third championship in four years by defeating

2. the Cleveland Cavaliers via a four-game _____ in the 2018 NBA Finals. Kevin Durant was

3. named the Most Valuable Player for his _____ performance in the four games that

4. they played. In a pivotal game, Durant scored 43 points and a _____ 3-point shot late

5. in the game to secure the win. Durant became the 11th player to win the award _____,

   winning in seasons 2017 and 2018.

C. Antonyms

Pick the word that means the opposite or near opposite of the word provided.

1.	**enmity**	hostility	antipathy	affection	antagonism	conflict
2.	**dented**	sunken	depressed	bulging	hollow	concave
3.	**gradient**	descent	incline	slant	slope	ramp
4.	**acquiesce**	dissent	accede	consent	yield	concur
5.	**deride**	ridicule	scoff	flout	revere	taunt
6.	**articulate**	enunciate	stammer	express	utter	verbalise
7.	**remnant**	whole	balance	remains	residue	leftovers
8.	**haggard**	emaciated	wasted	bony	fleshy	skinny

D. Missing letters

Fill in the missing letters to complete the word in the boxes below.

1. Bears are characterised by their | s | | o | | c | | y | body with round ears,

2. short tail and long square snout. They are among the | | a | | r | | e | s | |

3. carnivores on Earth. Bears are commonly seen in | s | | | r | | | m | s |

4. and wooded areas which are good sources of food. They usually eat trout, insects and even

| g | | r | b | | | e | which is left behind by campers or hikers. During winter,

5. bears slow down and go into a deep sleep known as | t | | | | p | | r | .

E. Homophones and homographs

Homophones are two or more words having the same pronunciation but different spellings and meanings. Homographs are words which have the same spelling but different meanings.

From the list below, fill in the blanks. (The first one has been done for you).

| moose | mousse | stake | steak | fall | waist | waste |

1. A ruminant mammal — moose
2. Trash; garbage — waste
3. The money put up by a gambler — stake
4. The season between summer and winter — fall
5. A slice of meat cut from a fleshy part of an animal — steak
6. A light spongy food containing cream or gelatine — mousse
7. Descend freely by the force of gravity — fall
8. A narrow part of the body between the hips and chest — waist

Set 4

A. Synonyms

Select the word that most closely matches the meaning of the word provided.

1.	**goad**	restraint	accept	provoke	discourage	dissuade
2.	**incredulity**	unbelief	credence	certitude	assurance	confidence
3.	**infatuation**	contempt	apathy	hatred	detachment	obsession
4.	**insatiable**	unmotivated	voracious	satisfied	gradual	fair
5.	**intrepid**	timid	yellow	cowardly	audacious	shy
6.	**inveterate**	confirmed	unusual	transient	brief	temporary
7.	**lithe**	stiff	awkward	flexible	rigid	stubborn

B. Fill in the blanks

Fill in the blanks from the words in the table below. There are two extra words you do not need.

upsets	undefeated	reached	latest	match	reigning	racket

1. Angelique Kerber and Petra Kritova became the _____ top players to be eliminated in the

2. ongoing US Open tennis championships in Armstrong Stadium. The _____ Wimbledon

3. champion, Kerber lost to Dominika Cibulkova. In the next _____, on court Aryna Sabalenka

4. defeated Kvitova. Just three of the top 10 seeds in the women's draw have _____ the

5. fourth round. These matches are just some of the _____ in this year's US Open.

C. Antonyms

Pick the word that means the opposite or near opposite of the word provided.

1.	**measly**	inferior	generous	little	petty	minute
2.	**lavish**	extravagant	extreme	frugal	fancy	luxurious
3.	**native**	home grown	local	domestic	immigrant	indigenous
4.	**potent**	powerless	strong	heavy	influential	effective
5.	**rejoice**	smile	grieve	delight	glory	triumph
6.	**vehement**	energetic	forceful	stoic	passionate	aggressive
7.	**tribute**	citation	honour	salutation	memorial	reprimand

D. Missing words

Choose the best word to complete the sentences.

Mangoes are fruits that comes from (1) _____ (same, different, one) species of tropical trees. Wild mangoes, which are the majority of these species, are found in (2) _____ (tropical, ocean, coastal) areas. Mango trees are (3) _____ (exported, native, rare) to South Asia but have been (4) _____ (found, given, distributed) worldwide to become one of the most widely (5) _____ (reared, cultivated, killed) fruits wherever the climate is suitable.

E. Odd one out

Four of the words in each list are linked. Mark the word that is not related to these four.

Example: red   green   ~~stripy~~   blue   yellow

1.	umbrella	raincoat	swimsuit	boots	jacket
2.	swim	surf	sun	snow	sand
3.	hotel	hospital	school	church	mountain
4.	snake	turtle	lizard	dolphin	crocodile
5.	table	chair	car	cabinet	desk

F. Idioms

Match each idiom to its meaning.

1.	**Barking up the wrong tree**	a. A situation that involves two people who are both responsible for it
2.	**Once in a blue moon**	b. A task that is easy or simple
3.	**A piece of cake**	c. Happens very rarely
4.	**Steal someone's thunder**	d. Making the wrong choice; following the wrong path
5.	**It takes two to tango**	e. Take credit for something someone else did

Set 5

A. Synonyms

Select the word that most closely matches the meaning of the word provided.

1.	**lurid**	modest	vivid	dull	boring	pleasing
2.	**myriad**	limited	calculable	measurable	innumerable	finite
3.	**nuanced**	subtle	direct	blatant	imprecise	factual
4.	**obsequious**	servile	disobedient	arrogant	assertive	rebellious
5.	**pallid**	florid	sickly	strong	colourful	flushed
6.	**peruse**	glance	glimpse	peek	look	scrutinise
7.	**beset**	defend	provide	plague	assist	aid
8.	**prodigious**	stupendous	microscopic	unexceptional	tiny	normal

B. Fill in the blanks

Fill in the blanks from the words in the table below. There are two extra words you do not need.

colonies	stones	wings	species	kinds	helpless	useful

1. Ants have more than 12,000 _____ all over the world. Ants are frustrating when they get

2. into our homes or when we are outside but they are _____ to the environment. They live in

3. large _____ which may consist of a million ants or more depending on the species. In a

4. colony there are three _____ of ants: the queen, female workers and males. Unlike

5. the queen and the male ants, the female workers do not have _____.

C. Antonyms

Pick the word that means the opposite or near opposite of the word provided.

1.	**pummel**	batter	thrash	strike	lambast	surrender
2.	**queer**	mainstream	peculiar	bizarre	curious	eccentric
3.	**arduous**	laborious	toilsome	straightforward	severe	hard
4.	**assiduous**	diligent	sedulous	industrious	negligent	tireless
5.	**subservient**	assertive	slavish	humble	obedient	servile
6.	**idiosyncratic**	peculiar	eccentric	abnormal	odd	conformist
7.	**heresy**	atheism	orthodoxy	nonconformity	dissidence	dissent
8.	**rigorously**	exactly	precisely	strictly	rigidly	loosely

D. Missing letters

Fill in the missing letters to complete the words in the boxes below.

1. Bees are flying insects `r _ l _ _ e d` to ants and wasps. They eat

2. nectar and pollen for their `_ n e _ g _` needs & other nutrient requirements.

3. Many bees collect pollen from a `_ a n _ e _` of flowering plants, but some

4. bees only gather pollen from one or a few species of `p _ a _ t _`.

5. The Indonesian Resin is the world's largest species of bee and the Dwarf Stingless is the `s _ _ l l _ s t`.

E. Homophones and homographs

Homophones are two or more words having the same pronunciation but different spellings and meanings. Homographs are words which have the same spelling but different meanings.

From the list below, fill in the blanks. (The first one has been done for you).

| spell | bark | sail | sale | wave |

1. Sound produced by a dog _____bark_____
2. To direct by a movement or gesture _____
3. Spoken words believed to have a magic power _____
4. A sequence of ridges that moves across a body of water or a liquid _____
5. An indefinite but usually short period of time _____
6. To travel across a body of water _____
7. Natural covering of a tree _____
8. The exchange of goods, services or property for a certain amount of money _____

Set 6

A. Synonyms

Select the word that most closely matches the meaning of the word provided.

1.	**plunder**	strip	give	deliver	gift	receive
2.	**perforate**	patch	puncture	plug	seal	fill
3.	**undermine**	bolster	strengthen	support	invigorate	sabotage
4.	**frenzied**	composed	insane	tranquil	placid	serene
5.	**turbid**	clear	luminous	colourless	cloudy	transparent
6.	**turbulent**	silent	furious	peaceful	tranquil	quiet
7.	**valiant**	cowardly	weak	fearful	gutless	courageous

B. Fill in the blanks

Fill in the blanks from the words in the table below. There are two extra words you do not need.

composed	gravity	divided	troposphere	absorbs	oxygen	carbon dioxide

1. The Earth's atmosphere is _____ of different gases such as nitrogen and carbon

2. dioxide. It also includes _____ which allows us to breath. The atmosphere

3. _____ some of the ultraviolet rays from the sun that could harm our skin and

4. cause sunburn. The atmosphere is _____ into five major layers. The first

5. layer, the _____, is the closest to the Earth's surface and almost all-weather changes

   occur in this layer.

C. Antonyms

Pick the word that means the opposite or near opposite of the word provided.

1.	**macabre**	gruesome	ghastly	lovely	horrible	grim
2.	**jubilant**	rejoicing	proud	depressed	triumphant	exultant
3.	**aboriginal**	foreign	native	primordial	primitive	indigenous
4.	**lofty**	tall	high	altitudinous	low	towering
5.	**connoisseur**	expert	aesthete	epicure	novice	master
6.	**scruple**	qualm	doubt	hesitation	waver	certainty
7.	**alliteration**	rhythm	dissonance	repetition	litany	recurrence

D Missing words

Choose the best word to complete the sentences.

George Washington (1) _____ (was, were, is) the first president of the United States. He was (2) _____ (conflictingly, contrastingly, unanimously) elected by the people on April 30, 1879. He is (3) _____ (labelled, known, tagged) for leading the victory of the American forces during the American War of Independence. He (4) _____ (recognised, implemented, lamented) the constitution written by the Founding Fathers which lays down the rules and regulations that Presidents still follow today. He was a very good leader and (5) _____ (lead, followed, led) the country for 8 peaceful years.

E. Odd one out

Four of the words in each list are linked. Mark the word that is not related to these four.

Example: red   green   ~~stripy~~   blue   yellow

1. basketball   volleyball   tennis   chess   football
2. horror   comedy   ballad   action   thriller
3. slippers   shoes   socks   gloves   boots
4. ball pen   paper   pencil   chalk   marker
5. roof   window   telephone   door   wall

F. Idioms

Match each idiom to its meaning.

1. **Add insult to injury**   a. Being in an undesirable situation that needs to be resolved by strong actions
2. **Cry over spilt milk**   b. To take shortcuts in order to complete tasks easily usually involving a compromise in safety or quality
3. **Drastic times call for drastic measures**   c. To worsen an unfavourable situation
4. **Cut corners**   d. Without any delay
5. **At the drop of a hat**   e. To be upset over something which cannot be fixed anymore

Set 7

A. Synonyms

Select the word that most closely matches the meaning of the word provided.

1.	**adhere**	loosen	cling	drop	fall	separate
2.	**feasible**	achievable	impossible	unlikely	impractical	far fetched
3.	**beacon**	black	light	dark	dull	obscure
4.	**beatitude**	misery	sadness	bliss	sorrow	agony
5.	**climax**	base	abyss	trough	bottom	pinnacle
6.	**cloudy**	colourless	murky	clear	transparent	filtered
7.	**delectable**	unpleasant	delightful	unpalatable	horrid	repulsive
8.	**succinct**	verbose	diffuse	wordy	concise	rambling

B. Fill in the blanks

Fill in the blanks from the words in the table below. There are two extra words you do not need.

hit	boat	liner	deemed	massive	voyage	unsinkable

1. The Titanic was a passenger _____ which sank on the morning of April 15, 1912. Titanic

2. was advertised as _____ which meant its owners claimed that it could not be

3. sunk. The Titanic was _____ to be the fastest and safest ship of its time.

4. Its maiden _____ was from England to France and finally to New York. However,

5. it _____ an iceberg on its fourth night, which laid the ship to its rest.

C. Antonyms

Pick the word that means the opposite or near opposite of the word provided.

1.	**eminent**	illustrious	noble	notable	insignificant	noteworthy
2.	**efface**	abolish	construct	eradicate	erase	liquidate
3.	**factual**	historical	objective	fictitious	true	literal
4.	**gumption**	backbone	insanity	initiative	sense	grit
5.	**incumbent**	office holder	occupant	obligatory	candidate	binding
6.	**gruesome**	awful	attractive	horrible	frightful	appalling
7.	**hiatus**	hiccup	interim	interval	interruption	continuation
8.	**emancipate**	liberate	incarcerate	deliver	discharge	release

D. Missing letters

Fill in the missing letters to complete the words in the boxes below.

1. Cinco de Mayo is celebrated to | h | o | | | | r | | how the Mexican

2. army | | e | f | | a | | | d | the French in the Battle of Puebla in 1862.

3. It is also a | c | | | m | | m | | | a | t | | | o | n | of

4. Mexican culture and heritage which includes | | a | | | | d | e | s |

5. and a re-enactment of the Battle of Puebla. However, Cinco de Mayo is not a

| f | | d | e | | | l | holiday, so offices, banks and stores stay open on this day.

E. Homophones and homographs

Homophones are two or more words having the same pronunciation but different spellings and meanings. Homographs are words which have the same spelling but different meanings.

From the list below, fill in the blanks. (The first one has been done for you).

| hair | hare | patient | kind | mine |

1. Swift, gnawing, herbivorous, mammals — hare
2. An individual under medical care and treatment — patient
3. Threadlike outgrowth in the skin of an animal — hair
4. Steadfast despite opposition or adversity — patient
5. A group united by common traits or interests — kind
6. Having a sympathetic or helpful nature — kind
7. A pit from which mineral substances are taken — mine
8. Used to imply possession or ownership — mine

Set 8

A. Synonyms

Select the word that most closely matches the meaning of the word provided.

1.	**zesty**	insipid	pungent	flat	flavourless	boring
2.	**yank**	drop	push	haul	shove	thrust
3.	**placate**	enrage	annoy	irritate	pacify	inflame
4.	**bemoan**	lament	rejoice	applaud	laugh	gloat
5.	**altruistic**	greedy	benevolent	egoistic	selfish	narcissistic
6.	**vagrant**	vagabond	resident	settled	static	citizen
7.	**vast**	midget	miniature	microscopic	minute	humongous

B. Fill in the blanks

Fill in the blanks from the words in the table below. There are two extra words you do not need.

ward	religion	tradition	include	before	attract	originated

1. Halloween is celebrated during the night _____ All Saints' Day. It is a

2. _____ to dress up in scary costumes such as ghosts, cartoon characters, pirates,

3. and witches during this night. Activities _____ trick and treat and carving of

4. pumpkins. The Halloween tradition _____ from the Celtic festival of Samhain where

5. people wear costumes and make noises to _____ off evil spirits.

C. Antonyms

Pick the word that means the opposite or near opposite of the word provided.

1.	**astute**	gullible	shrewd	intelligent	perceptive	clever
2.	**tame**	boring	domesticated	dull	dreary	wild
3.	**candour**	frankness	integrity	artifice	honesty	veracity
4.	**sagging**	drooping	upright	bowing	descending	hanging
5.	**curtail**	diminish	prolong	contract	abbreviate	limit
6.	**conscientious**	scrupulous	meticulous	particular	thorough	careless
7.	**melancholy**	delighted	disconsolate	glum	morose	forlorn

D. Missing words

Choose the best word to complete the sentences.

The young Albert Einstein was unable to talk until he reached the age of four. He was

(1) _____ (expelled, entered, paddled) from school at an early age. But as a young genius,

he (2) _____ (loved, loves, love) mathematics and science. He was (3)

_____ (labelled, awarded, bought) the Nobel Prize for Physics in 1921. His most famous

(4) _____ (answer, equation, question) is $E = mc^2$. He (5) _____ (taught,

thought, taunt) Physics in New Jersey until his death on April 18, 1955.

E. Odd one out

Four of the words in each list are linked. Mark the word that is not related to these four.

Example: red   green   ~~stripy~~   blue   yellow

1.	ocean	stream	river	valley	lake
2.	car	truck	bicycle	jeep	bus
3.	apple	cabbage	orange	pear	grapes
4.	cat	lion	dog	panther	tiger
5.	water	coffee	lemonade	soft drinks	cake

F. Idioms

Match each idiom to its meaning.

1. **Fall between two stools**
2. **Best of both worlds**
3. **Beat around the bush**
4. **Far cry from**
5. **Don't put all your eggs in one basket**

a. To have two positive options and be able to accept both of them.

b. Do not put all your resources into one possibility

c. Very different from something else

d. To have two options and not be able to accommodate either of them

e. Avoid the main topic; waste time

Set 9

A. Synonyms

Select the word that most closely matches the meaning of the word provided.

1.	**sanguine**	pessimistic	negative	depressed	optimistic	dubious
2.	**succumb**	capitulate	endure	conquer	survive	overcome
3.	**wayward**	manageable	biddable	capricious	compliant	obedient
4.	**palatable**	flat	appetising	flavourless	insipid	unsavoury
5.	**blustery**	peaceful	stormy	breezy	serene	calm
6.	**clamorous**	vociferous	silent	hushed	tranquil	humble
7.	**inspect**	skim	overlook	neglect	ignore	examine
8.	**deteriorate**	recover	recuperate	degenerate	ameliorate	mend

B. Fill in the blanks

Fill in the blanks from the words in the table below. There are two extra words you do not need.

border	glaciers	incapable	highest	inhabited	summit	snow

1. Mount Everest is the _____ point on earth above sea level. It is shaped like a

2. three-sided pyramid and serves as a _____ between Nepal and China.

3. Large _____ cover the slopes of Mount Everest. The valleys

4. found below the mountain are _____ by Tibetan-speaking people. The weather on

5. the _____ of the mountain is so severe and there is so little oxygen that it is and

   uninhabitable.

C. Antonyms

Pick the word that means the opposite or near opposite of the word provided.

1.	**vulgar**	foul	filthy	decent	gross	crude
2.	**voluptuous**	fleshy	lush	sensual	sensuous	ascetic
3.	**maven**	apprentice	expert	genius	adept	whiz
4.	**tardy**	behind	overdue	punctual	delinquent	late
5.	**colloquial**	vernacular	chatty	literary	familiar	slang
6.	**chivalrous**	gallant	courtly	noble	brutish	considerate
7.	**congenial**	obnoxious	pleasant	amiable	affable	cordial
8.	**conundrum**	enigma	mystery	answer	riddle	dilemma

D. Missing letters

Fill in the missing letters to complete the words in the boxes below.

1. There are many ways to | e | l | | | i | n | | t | | waste and protect

2. the environment. You could | | e | | s | e | things again instead of throwing

3. them away. Another way is to | r | | d | | | e | consumption which may

4. be done by using resources wisely. Finally, you could | | e | c | | | l | e |

5. trash and transform it into new products. Practicing the 3 R's of waste management will help us

| m | a | | n | | | i | | a healthy environment.

E. Homophones and homographs

Homophones are two or more words having the same pronunciation but different spellings and meanings. Homographs are words which have the same spelling but different meanings.

From the list below, fill in the blanks. (The first one has been done for you).

| loan | lone | lap | like | bat |

1. Money which has to be paid back usually with interest _____loan_____
2. One complete trip around a race track _____
3. Possessing characteristics that are the same or almost the same _____
4. A wooden club used to strike the ball _____
5. To find someone or something pleasant or attractive _____
6. Front area of the thighs of a seated person _____
7. Having no company _____
8. A flying mammal _____

Set 10

A. Synonyms

Select the word that most closely matches the meaning of the word provided.

1.	**apocalypse**	godsend	catastrophe	manna	genesis	blessing
2.	**apprehend**	discharge	liberate	free	arrest	release
3.	**borderline**	central	middle	frontier	internal	inner
4.	**bothersome**	delightful	pleasing	insignificant	negligible	disturbing
5.	**emulate**	echo	spurn	condemn	divest	convey
6.	**coerce**	allow	permit	convince	force	induce
7.	**discrepancy**	likeness	difference	resemblance	sameness	similarity

B. Fill in the blanks

Fill in the blanks from the words in the table below. There are two extra words you do not need.

drift	surface	incorporated	geologists	fossils	palaeontologists	crust

1. A long time ago, all the continents of the world were _____ in one big

2. supercontinent called Pangaea. _____ from several species of plants and animals have been found in different modern continents which were once joined together in Pangaea.

3. _____ also have found similar types of rock across the present continents. The

4. continents are part of the Earth's _____, which is the outer surface of the Earth.

5. Over millions of years, the Earth's plates moved, causing the Pangaea to _____ apart.

C. Antonyms

Pick the word that means the opposite or near opposite of the word provided.

1.	**dynamic**	energetic	stagnant	robust	vigorous	vital
2.	**dwell**	abide	remain	escape	stay	tarry
3.	**exquisite**	fine	elegant	dainty	crude	sublime
4.	**domicile**	habitat	public	residence	dwelling	lodging
5.	**copious**	niggardly	plentiful	abundant	affluent	extensive
6.	**subsidy**	subvention	allowance	support	assistance	tax
7.	**gutsy**	cowardly	daring	audacious	bold	adventurous

D. Missing words

Choose the best word to complete the sentences.

Zeus was the king of the Greek gods. He was (1) _____ (known, knew, know) as the god of sky and thunder. He was famously known to have the (2) _____ (secret, gadget, ability) to throw lightning bolts. He could also (3) _____ (call, control, talk) the weather, causing rain and storms. Whenever Zeus travelled, he went in (4) _____ (disguise, horse, car) so that the mortals would not recognise him. He was also known to be (5) _____ (unrecognizable, unpredictable, undecided), as no one was able to guess the decisions that he would make.

E. Odd one out

Four of the words in each list are linked. Mark the word that is not related to these four.

Example: red   green   ~~stripy~~   blue   yellow

1.	clouds	moon	sun	plane	stars
2.	eagle	parrot	bat	pigeon	owl
3.	ship	raft	car	boat	jet ski
4.	gold	ivory	silver	copper	lead
5.	saunter	amble	run	sprint	nod

F. Idioms

Match each idiom to its meaning.

1. **Play devil's advocate**

2. **A penny for your thoughts**

3. **Cross that bridge when (one) comes to it**

4. **Cut the mustard**

5. **Don't count your chickens before they're hatched**

a. A way of asking what someone is thinking

b. Don't make plans for future events that might not happen

c. Always contradict or argue against a given idea or suggestion

d. To deal with a problem when it actually happens or becomes an issue

e. Perform satisfactorily; come up to expectations

Set 11

A. Synonyms

Select the word that most closely matches the meaning of the word provided.

1.	**gullible**	streetwise	sceptical	naive	wary	cynical
2.	**guile**	honesty	cunning	artlessness	sincerity	ingenuousness
3.	**hysteria**	peacefulness	quiet	serenity	agitation	tranquillity
4.	**multifaceted**	simple	trivial	versatile	obvious	unvarying
5.	**interfere**	disregard	intrude	ignore	neglect	avoid
6.	**insult**	affront	compliment	acclaim	praise	glorify
7.	**jest**	earnest	grave	quip	solemn	sober
8.	**jeopardy**	security	protection	danger	safety	defence

B. Fill in the blanks

Fill in the blanks from the words in the table below. There are two extra words you do not need.

popular	equipment	different	class	similar	catch	throw

1. Rugby is a game _____ to football. Just like other ball games, the

2. _____ used to play rugby is a ball, similar to a football, but with rounded ends.

3. The ball is made of leather which makes it easy to throw and _____. Rugby

4. players and fans are mostly from upper and middle _____ backgrounds.

5. Rugby is now becoming a _____ sport in many countries around the world.

C. Antonyms

Pick the word that means the opposite or near opposite of the word provided.

1.	**kindred**	akin	affiliated	unrelated	allied	associated
2.	**supposition**	assumption	proof	hypothesis	conjecture	guess
3.	**lucid**	clear	brilliant	confusing	coherent	logical
4.	**hanker**	want	hunger	pine	desire	averse
5.	**annihilated**	preserved	eradicated	eliminated	obliterated	liquidated
6.	**clandestine**	open	covert	concealed	furtive	stealthy
7.	**dearth**	paucity	plethora	shortage	famine	insufficiency
8.	**obsolete**	outdated	moribund	antiquated	modern	antique

D. Missing letters

Fill in the missing letters to complete the words in the boxes below.

1. The Bermuda Triangle remains one of the | m | y | | | e | r | | e | |

2. of the world. Many ships and planes have | | i | s | p | | e | | r | d |

3. in this area. Popular theories | a | | | r | | b | | t | e | the

4. mysteries to extra-terrestrial beings. However, there is no | p | | o | | f |

5. In fact, some people can still | | | v | | g | | t | e | around the

Bermuda Triangle unharmed.

E. Homophones and homographs

Homophones are two or more words having the same pronunciation but different spellings and meanings. Homographs are words which have the same spelling but different meanings.

From the list below, fill in the blanks. (The first one has been done for you).

| incite | insight | pound | firm | count |

1. To move to action — _____incite_____
2. The basic monetary unit of the United Kingdom — _____
3. Not easily moved or disturbed — _____
4. To recite or indicate the numbers in order — _____
5. A form of business organisation — _____
6. A unit of weight equal to 16 ounces — _____
7. The ability to understand or know the true nature of a situation — _____
8. Used as a title for a nobleman — _____

Set 12

A. Synonyms

Select the word that most closely matches the meaning of the word.

1.	**obstacle**	break	advantage	hindrance	boost	benefit
2.	**facetious**	serious	comical	solemn	grave	earnest
3.	**pleasurable**	irritating	annoying	upsetting	unpleasant	delectable
4.	**fatuous**	absurd	clever	astute	ingenious	discerning
5.	**quench**	extinguish	fire	ignite	inflame	light
6.	**quirky**	bizarre	average	standard	typical	usual
7.	**rampant**	bridled	uncontrolled	checked	hampered	hindered

B. Fill in the blanks

Fill in the blanks from the words in the table below. There are two extra words you do not need.

accord	immigrant	monarch	head	king	ruled	celebrated

1. Queen Elizabeth II has _____ the United Kingdom for a very long time.

2. She _____ her 65th year on the throne in February 2017. She is the first

3. British _____ to have reached a Sapphire Jubilee. Over the years, she has tried to

4. modernise the monarchy in _____ with changes in society. Queen

5. Elizabeth is the longest-reigning living queen and female _____ of state.

C. Antonyms

Pick the word that means the opposite or near opposite of the word provided.

1.	**robust**	strong	fit	healthy	hale	ailing
2.	**inane**	asinine	vacuous	ludicrous	sensible	idiotic
3.	**convivial**	distant	festive	jocund	friendly	genial
4.	**deferential**	subservient	docile	humble	contemptuous	civil
5.	**twine**	string	rope	straighten	twist	cord
6.	**sequentially**	numerically	successively	continually	consecutively	intermittently
7.	**shabby**	natty	dilapidated	scruffy	tatty	ragged

D. Missing words

Choose the best word to complete the sentences.

Global warming is (1) _____ (define, defined, defining) as the increase in the Earth's average temperature. One major (2) _____ (cause, effect, product) of global warming is the accumulation of greenhouse gases. Greenhouse gases such as carbon dioxide and ozone are (3) _____ (trapped, escaped, vaporized) in the Earth's atmosphere causing the Earth to warm up. In our own little ways, we can help (4) _____ (hasten, stir, prevent) global warming by using less electricity. (5) _____ (Watering, Loving, Planting) trees also helps a lot as they absorb carbon dioxide from the atmosphere.

E. Odd one out

Four of the words in each list are linked. Mark the word that is not related to these four.

Example: red   green   ~~stripy~~   blue   yellow

1.	cottage	bungalow	villa	farm	mansion
2.	table	chair	refrigerator	desk	cupboard
3.	ear	lip	cheek	chest	nose
4.	mouse	tree	man	stone	bird
5.	radio	television	printer	umbrella	laptop

F. Idioms

Match each idiom to its meaning.

1.	**Make a long story short**	a. Reveal a secret
2.	**Let the cat out of the bag**	b. Leave a situation as it is so as not to worsen it
3.	**Keep something at bay**	c. Having no manners
4.	**Let sleeping dogs lie**	d. To leave out parts of a story; to give a brief summary
5.	**Not a spark of decency**	e. Distance one's self from something harmful or dangerous

Set 13

A. Synonyms

Select the word that most closely matches the meaning of the word provided.

1.	**meagre**	ample	extensive	scanty	bottomless	enormous
2.	**unorthodox**	norm	queer	traditional	standard	customary
3.	**malady**	disorder	treatment	remedy	healing	comfort
4.	**beleaguered**	harassed	defended	aided	supported	alleviated
5.	**ornate**	plain	modest	simple	bare	elaborate
6.	**foe**	buddy	ally	opponent	colleague	accomplice
7.	**garish**	classy	muted	vulgar	subdued	prudent
8.	**deterrent**	hindrance	catalyst	stimulus	motive	driver

B. Fill in the blanks

Fill in the blanks from the words in the table below. There are two extra words you do not need.

improving	originated	exports	tropical	rich	fruit	rank

1. Bananas _____ from the Indo-Malaysian region before conquering the world.

2. Bananas grow in _____ countries. They are the fourth largest fruit crop in the

3. world, and also one of the largest _____ of the Philippines. Bananas

4. are said to be _____ in fibre and potassium. Eating bananas brings several health

5. benefits, such as _____ the condition of the heart and minimizing health

   risks.

C. Antonyms

Pick the word that means the opposite or near opposite of the word provided.

1.	**forged**	fabricated	counterfeit	invented	falsified	authentic
2.	**yield**	submit	give in	resist	resign	succumb
3.	**apprehensive**	nervous	worried	jittery	dauntless	upset
4.	**notion**	fact	idea	concept	suspicion	theory
5.	**meticulous**	negligent	scrupulous	accurate	painstaking	rigorous
6.	**austere**	severe	harsh	frivolous	stringent	rigorous
7.	**taut**	snug	slack	rigid	unyielding	tight
8.	**menial**	servile	arrogant	humble	abject	ignoble

D. Missing letters

Fill in the missing letters to complete the words in the boxes below.

1. Dogs are [_ | n | _ | w | _ | n] as man's best friend. They have a very good

2. [s | _ | _ | s | e] of smell which makes them very useful for tracking bombs and

3. illegal drugs. They also have [s | _ | _ | s | i | _ | i | v | _] ears making

4. them good guard dogs. Dogs can also read [_ | m | o | _ | i | _ | n | _] '

5. feelings and facial expressions, which is the reason why they are considered to be great

[c | _ | m | p | _ | n | _ | o | _ | _] .

E. Homophones and homographs

Homophones are two or more words having the same pronunciation but different spellings and meanings. Homographs are words which have the same spelling but different meanings.

From the list below, fill in the blanks. (The first one has been done for you).

bill	reign	rain	scale	project

1. Water falling in droplets from the atmosphere   _____rain_____
2. To throw or thrust forward   _____
3. A list of items bought and their prices   _____
4. A specific plan or design for accomplishing something _____
5. A period during which a monarch rules   _____
6. An instrument or machine for weighing   _____
7. Jaws of a bird together with their horny covering   _____
8. Part of the external body covering of a fish   _____

Set 14

A. Synonyms

Select the word that most closely matches the meaning of the word.

1.	**coax**	wheedle	impose	discourage	front	coerce
2.	**conceal**	divulge	unveil	flaunt	shroud	confess
3.	**consider**	guess	gamble	deliberate	hope	speculate
4.	**curb**	control	foster	broaden	enliven	support
5.	**destitute**	moneyed	wealthy	indigent	prosperous	posh
6.	**dilute**	strengthen	debase	condense	intensify	thicken
7.	**elude**	confront	follow	pursue	obtrude	evade

B. Fill in the blanks

Fill in the blanks from the words in the table below.

natives	sea	tourists	atoll	Ocean	vegetation	region

1. The Maldives is a ring-shaped _____, made up of a group of coral islands. The country

2. is well known for its white beaches and the warms waters of the Indian _____. The

3. islands are inhabited by almost 300,000 _____ who are joined by large numbers of

4. _____ - every year. The Maldives is one of the world's most geographically dispersed

5. sovereign states and the smallest Asian country. Coconut trees dominates its tropical _____

but banana and papaya trees can also be seen there.

C. Antonyms

Pick the word that means the opposite or near opposite of the word provided.

1.	**famine**	starvation	feast	drought	paucity	scarcity
2.	**feeble**	frail	weak	debilitated	potent	infirm
3.	**hoax**	real	swindle	con	fraud	bamboozle
4.	**impudent**	impertinent	demure	brazen	presumptuous	cheeky
5.	**lenient**	tolerant	charitable	severe	mild	flexible
6.	**nimble**	agile	clumsy	sprightly	brisk	fleet
7.	**obstinate**	stubborn	compliant	firm	determined	adamant

D. Missing words

Choose the best word to complete the sentences.

In ancient Greece Hercules was very popular because of his great (1) _____ (strength, weakness, clumsiness) and intelligence. He was a (2) _____ (demigod, human, ruler), the son of Zeus and Alcmene, a mortal. However, his mother (3) _____ (grew, raised, sees) him as a normal child. He had a lot of talents but he had (4) _____ (difficulty, grudge, feelings) in learning music. He became a powerful (5) _____ (warrior, soldier, sorcerer) and a hero because he always saved the people from trouble.

E. Odd one out

Four of the words in each list are linked. Mark the word that is not related to these four.

Example: red   green   ~~stripy~~   blue   yellow

1.	frog	crab	fish	tortoise	toad
2.	square	rectangle	circle	rhombus	pentagon
3.	antagonist	opponent	ally	adversary	enemy
4.	guitar	piano	radio	violin	drums
5.	pesos	dollars	euros	ounces	pounds

F. Idioms

Match each idiom to its meaning.

1.	**The greatest thing since sliced bread**	a. To stay up late at night working or studying
2.	**The ball is in your court**	b. To hear rumours about something or someone
3.	**Every cloud has a silver lining**	c. The best and most innovative idea or invention for a long time
4.	**To Hear it through the grapevine**	d. A negative or difficult situation may have a positive outcome or may become beneficial in the end
5.	**To burn the midnight oil**	e. It is up to you to make the next decision or step

Set 15

A. Synonyms

Select the word that most closely matches the meaning of the word provided.

1.	**polarised**	alike	similar	contradictory	identical	convergent
2.	**matte**	dull	lustrous	glossy	bright	polished
3.	**immerse**	douse	dry	shower	rain	float
4.	**enterprise**	indolence	apathy	idleness	venture	passivity
5.	**temperate**	immoderate	restrained	stubborn	uninhibited	severe
6.	**puncture**	pierce	sew	fix	patch	inflate
7.	**oppress**	free	liberate	suppress	exhilarate	relieve
8.	**pretence**	actuality	humility	truth	fact	hypocrisy

B. Fill in the blanks

Fill in the blanks from the words in the table below. There are two extra words you do not need.

done	tombs	man-made	built	unsurpassed	ruler	monument

1. The Great Pyramid of Giza was _____ for the Egyptian Pharaoh Khufu. A

2. pharaoh was the _____ of Egypt in ancient times. The ancient Egyptians

3. believed in the afterlife and the pyramids were built as _____ for the pharaohs.

4. For many years, the Great Pyramid of Giza was the tallest _____ structure in

   the world and is regarded as one of the seven wonders of the ancient world. Even now, its

5. height is _____ by anything built in Egypt.

C. Antonyms

Pick the word that means the opposite or near opposite of the word provided.

1.	**harbour**	protect	turn in	accommodate	lodge	house
2.	**trifling**	significant	irrelevant	trivial	inessential	minor
3.	**tyrant**	bully	despot	autocrat	authoritarian	democrat
4.	**deceit**	guile	fraud	cheating	candour	cunning
5.	**endeavour**	attempt	strive	surrender	try	struggle
6.	**ordeal**	tribulation	affliction	torment	pleasure	anguish
7.	**elucidate**	befuddle	explain	illuminate	interpret	enlighten
8.	**revive**	restore	renew	kill	block	organisation

D. Missing Letters

Fill in the missing letters to complete the words in the boxes below.

1. The Amazon is the world's biggest | a | | i | | f | | | e | | s | | .

2. It | c | | m | p | | | s | | s | 40% of the land area of Brazil.

3. The Amazon is the most varied | e | | | s | | s | t | | | on

4. earth containing several million species. It is | i | | p | | | t | | n |

5. because the vegetation in the rainforest can | | b | s | | | b | 140 million tons of

carbon dioxide emitted from the atmosphere.

E. Homophones and homographs

Homophones are two or more words having the same pronunciation but different spellings and meanings. Homographs are words which have the same spelling but different meanings.

From the list below, fill in the blanks. (The first one has been done for you).

| soul | sole | crane | ring | minute |

1. The spiritual principle embodied in human beings   _____soul_____
2. A rectangular area used for sports such as boxing or wrestling   _____
3. Being the only one   _____
4. A unit of time equivalent to 60 seconds   _____
5. A machine for raising, shifting, and lowering heavy weights   _____
6. Exceptionally small or of small importance   _____
7. A circular object usually made of precious metal worn on the finger   _____
8. A tall wading bird having a long neck, long legs and long bill which lives in the marshes and plains   _____

Set 16

A. Synonyms

Select the word that most closely matches the meaning of the word provided.

1.	**barren**	full	productive	arid	fruitful	developing
2.	**peril**	hazard	haven	safety	security	asylum
3.	**fleet**	slow	hasty	tardy	sluggish	lethargic
4.	**commence**	cease	inaugurate	conclude	stop	terminate
5.	**nomadic**	settled	rootless	permanent	fixed	rooted
6.	**explicate**	confuse	bemuse	obscure	unravel	complicate
7.	**insolent**	servile	humble	decent	gracious	impudent

B. Fill in the blanks

Fill in the blanks from the words in the table below. There are two extra words you do not need.

protect	dorsal	ability	combination	anchor	hermaphrodites	vertical

1. In the movie Finding Nemo, Nemo is an imaginary _____ of a clownfish and a sea

2. anemone. Clownfish have round tails and _____ fins which contains 11 spines.

3. They are commonly found together with anemones, which _____ themselves to

4. the sea floor. Clownfish contain a layer of mucus to _____ themselves from the

5. toxins anemones produce. All anemone fish, including clownfish, are _____,

    which means they are born as males, and when they mature, they turn into females.

C. Antonyms

Pick the word that means the opposite or near opposite of the word provided.

1. **recondite**   arcane   obscure   simple   occult   profound
2. **asunder**   separate   tear   unite   connect   rip
3. **queasy**   nauseous   satisfied   sick   squeamish anxious
4. **tranquil**   jittery   placid   pacific   quiet   serene
5. **prevaricate**   equivocate evade   dodge   be blunt   hedge
6. **complaisant**   cordial   belligerent affable   contented amiable
7. **altitude**   elevation top   apex   peak   valley

D. Missing words

Choose the best word to complete the sentences.

The Giant Sequoia is a (1) _____ (minute, massive, average) species of tree. These trees are (2) _____ (seen, saw, sawn) in the California Sierra Nevada mountain range. Giant Sequoia trees are an ancient species. In fact, the oldest known Giant Sequoia (3) _____ (fell, found, belongs) to the Jurassic Period which was almost 200 million years ago. The Sierra Nevada region experiences heavy rainfall. That is why the Giant Sequoia trees thrive there. They need a (4) _____ (slight, tremendous, scant) amount of water in order to thrive. One of the first Giant Sequoia, named the Discovery Tree, was (5) _____ (felled, fallen, felt) in 1853.

E. Odd one out

Four of the words in each list are linked. Mark the word that is not related to these four.

Example: red   green   ~~stripy~~   blue   yellow

1.	algebra	geometry	biology	calculus	trigonometry
2.	crocodile	snake	hen	rabbit	turtle
3.	knife	fork	spoon	stove	chopsticks
4.	dog	cat	wolf	rabbit	parrot
5.	chilli	ginger	sugar	pepper	garlic

F. Idioms

Match each idiom to its meaning.

1. **Not playing with a full deck**   a. To hear something from a reliable or the original source
2. **Wouldn't be caught dead**   b. To have no idea, do not know the answer to a question
3. **Your guess is as good as mine**   c. To miss a chance or opportunity
4. **Straight from the horse's mouth**   d. Someone who lacks intelligence; crazy
5. **Miss the boat**   e. Would never like to do something as discussed

Set 17

A. Synonyms

Select the word that most closely matches the meaning of the word that has been provided.

1.	**enervated**	debilitated	energetic	vigorous	dynamic	invigorated
2.	**nugatory**	significant	worthy	trivial	effective	impactful
3.	**quaff**	spit	eject	imbibe	refuse	throw up
4.	**mound**	ditch	valley	hillock	basin	canyon
5.	**panacea**	poison	venom	remedy	toxin	illness
6.	**pander**	gratify	refuse	deny	frustrate	dissatisfy
7.	**shudder**	steady	tremble	calm	stable	firm
8.	**vivid**	dull	murky	fuzzy	vague	picturesque

B. Fill in the blanks

Fill in the blanks from the words in the table below. There are two extra words you do not need.

corolla	extinction	group	lack	possess	parasitic	known

1. The largest flower _____ to the world is called Rafflesia. It gets its nutrients
2. from another living plant, making it a _____ plant. It is one of the rarest plants
3. in the world and is near _____. Rafflesia flowers are unisexual which means
4. they _____ either a stamen or carpel but never both. This flower is famously
5. known for its rotten smell due to a tentacle found inside the _____ of petals.

C. Antonyms

Pick the word that means the opposite or near opposite of the word provided.

1.	**pliant**	yielding	adamant	tractable	susceptible	supple
2.	**docile**	submissive	obedient	compliant	amenable	defiant
3.	**sedulous**	diligent	assiduous	persistent	negligent	dedicated
4.	**avow**	repudiate	assert	declare	affirm	aver
5.	**bemused**	bewildered	lost	confidant	confounded	bewildered
6.	**brusque**	gracious	abrupt	blunt	bluff	gruff
7.	**sybaritic**	luxurious	abstemious	voluptuous	sensual	hedonistic
8.	**turpitude**	righteousness	depravity	baseness	corruption	degradation

D. Missing Letters

Fill in the missing letters to complete the words in the boxes below.

1. The Ostrich is the tallest and largest b _ r _ _ in the world. It is a flightless bird,

2. however, they can _ t r _ d _ with their long legs. When they

3. sense danger their f _ _ t h _ r _ blend with the colours

4. of the sand. A group of ostriches is called a _ _ e r _ and contains 12 birds

5. Each group always has d _ m _ _ a _ t male and female leaders.

E. Homophones and homographs

Homophones are two or more words having the same pronunciation but different spellings and meanings. Homographs are words which have the same spelling but different meanings.

From the list below, fill in the blanks. (The first one has been done for you).

| canvas | canvass | object | contract | palms |

1. To oppose or disapprove of an idea or suggestion   _____object_____
2. Trees growing in tropical and subtropical regions with large feather-like or fan-shaped leaves   _____
3. To solicit votes from people   _____
4. Inner surface of the hands from the wrist to fingers   _____
5. To reduce in amount or quantity; to shrink   _____
6. An agreement between two or more persons or parties   _____
7. A piece of cloth backed or framed as a surface for a painting   _____
8. The goal or purpose of an effort or activity   _____

Set 18

A. Synonyms

Select the word that most closely matches the meaning of the word provided.

1. **abide**   breach   violate   comply   ignore   refuse
2. **abrade**   smoothen   level   flatten   scrape   plane
3. **abatement**   rehabilitation diminution   growth   extension   increase
4. **clemency**   forgiveness   cruelty   bloodlust   atrocity   harshness
5. **compel**   coax   deter   free   impede   coerce
6. **brevity**   conciseness   prolixity   longevity   verbosity   elongation
7. **callow**   experienced   naive   well-versed   mature   sophisticated

B. Fill in the blanks

Fill in the blanks from the words in the table below. There are two extra words you do not need.

plumage	flap	smaller	body	larger	habitat	native

1. The Bee Hummingbird is _____ to Cuba, an island in the Caribbean. It is
2. the smallest bird in the world, although the female is _____ than the male bird.
3. The Bee Hummingbird can _____ its wings between 80 and 200 times per second.
4. The _____ of these birds is in mature forests and forest edges. The upper
5. _____ of the Bee Hummingbird is bluish, while the rest is mostly greyish-white.

C. Antonyms

Pick the word that means the opposite or near opposite of the word provided.

1.	**camaraderie**	fellowship	solitude	friendship	association	company
2.	**cajole**	persuade	flatter	entice	repel	lure
3.	**cache**	store	hoard	absence	reserve	stock
4.	**scoundrel**	hero	cheat	rogue	crook	impostor
5.	**dawdle**	rush	linger	loiter	lag	delay
6.	**daft**	crazy	clever	mad	insane	deranged
7.	**discern**	distinguish	know	neglect	recognise	descry

D. Missing words

Choose the best word to complete the sentences.

Kiwis are flightless birds (1) _____ (foreign, unknown, native) outside New Zealand.

Kiwi birds do not have a (2) _____ (sternum, clavicle, mandible) or breastbone but they have strong legs. Kiwis are regarded as the unique (3) _____ (picture, symbol, caricature) of New Zealand. Kiwis is used as a (4) _____ (ball, logo, goal) for their rugby team also called the all blacks after the colour of their shirts. In foreign currency trading, the New Zealand dollar is also (5) _____ (unusually, surprisingly, commonly) known as "the Kiwi".

E. Odd one out

Four of the words in each list are linked. Mark the word that is not related to these four.

Example: red   green   ~~stripy~~   blue   yellow

1.	carrot	spinach	cabbage	guava	cauliflower
2.	indigo	pink	red	yellow	green
3.	lamb	kitten	goat	puppy	calf
4.	pitcher	bucket	glass	knife	bottle
5.	valley	hill	river	mountain	dam

F. Idioms

Match each idiom to its meaning.

1.	**To take with a pinch of salt**	a. The final problem that causes someone to lose patience
2.	**See eye to eye**	b. Experiencing the same unpleasant thing or harm you have done to others
3.	**The last straw**	c. To consider a statement, story or explanation more carefully especially when it comes from an unreliable source
4.	**To sit on the fence**	d. When two or more people agree on something
5.	**A Taste of your own medicine**	e. To avoid taking sides or making a decision

Set 19

A. Synonyms

Select the word that most closely matches the meaning of the word provided.

1.	**dwindle**	expand	enlarge	extend	accumulate	diminish
2.	**drudgery**	fun	grind	pleasure	relaxation	idleness
3.	**dunce**	nerd	genius	prodigy	fool	thinker
4.	**dreary**	happy	dismal	cheerful	glorious	pleasing
5.	**exult**	grieve	mourn	rejoice	lament	despair
6.	**foment**	provoke	soothe	allay	tranquilize	abate
7.	**guffaw**	sob	moan	laugh	groan	howl
8.	**rapacious**	charitable	generous	selfless	bountiful	avaricious

B. Fill in the blanks

Fill in the blanks from the words in the table below. There are two extra words you do not need.

ratified	earthquakes	record	withstand	revenue	construction	situated

1. The world's longest bridge, between Danyang and Kunshand, is _____ in East China.

It connects Shanghai with Nanjing. The final draft for the bridge's design was

2. _____ in early 2006. 10,000 people working for four years were needed for the

3. _____ of the grand bridge which was completed on November 15, 2010. It was

4. designed to _____ natural disasters such as typhoons, floods and

5. _____.

C. Antonyms

Pick the word that means the opposite or near opposite of the word provided.

1.	**hifalutin**	pretentious	humble	grandiose	pompous	haughty
2.	**interdiction**	embargo	entitlement	restraint	veto	taboo
3.	**insurgency**	rebellion	mutiny	uprising	loyalty	sedition
4.	**inundated**	flooded	deluged	immersed	parched	swamped
5.	**jaunty**	debonair	depressed	cheerful	lively	sprightly
6.	**coy**	brazen	coquettish	modest	timid	demure
7.	**covert**	hidden	furtive	conspicuous	surreptitious	clandestine
8.	**curt**	brusque	brief	bluff	laconic	lengthy

D. Missing letters

Fill in the missing letters to complete the words in the boxes below.

1. The Hawksbill Sea Turtle is the first biofluorescent   `r _ _ p _ _ l e`   discovered. Biofluorescence means that the light absorbed is from an

2. `_ u t _ _ i _ d _` source. This is different from bioluminescent. wherein

3. the light `_ o u _ c _` is in the body. Bio fluorescence is the turtle's

4. mechanism to `a _ t r _ c _` its prey. It is also believed that this is

5. camouflage as Hawksbill turtles are famous for `s _ _ e _ _ t _`

E. Homophones and homographs

Homophones are two or more words having the same pronunciation but different spellings and meanings. Homographs are words which have the same spelling but different meanings.

From the list below, fill in the blanks. (The first one has been done for you).

| week | weak | cabinet | chest | pen |

1. A case or cupboard usually having doors and shelves — _____cabinet_____
2. A period of seven days — _____
3. A box used for storage or transport — _____
4. An enclosure for animals — _____
5. A state where someone lacks strength or force — _____
6. A common writing instrument using ink — _____
7. A body of persons assigned by the head of state to lead various departments of the government or to act as advisers — _____
8. The part of the human body between the neck and abdomen — _____

Set 20

A. Synonyms

Select the word that most closely matches the meaning of the word provided.

1.	**depot**	arsenal	accommodation	shop	home	barracks
2.	**lucrative**	loss making	unprofitable	damaging	bankrupt	remunerative
3.	**lopsided**	askew	balanced	level	even	impartial
4.	**derelict**	overachiever	outcast	careful	superstar	beloved
5.	**ghastly**	pleasing	lovely	pretty	frightful	decent
6.	**dilapidated**	new	mended	shabby	repaired	improved
7.	**disarray**	organised	orderly	structured	tidy	clutter

B. Fill in the blanks

Fill in the blanks from the words in the table below. There are two extra words you do not need.

attached	amphibian	insects	mammal	underside	beneath	tropical

1. Diane's Bare-hearted Glass Frog is a/an _____ with a transparent skin on

2. its belly. You can see the frog's organs _____ its skin, particularly its heart. It

3. prefers to live in _____ forests. One frog can lay 20-30 eggs at one time and

4. these eggs are usually seen on the _____ of the leaves hanging over a

   body of water. Unlike other frogs, Diane's Glass Frogs stay with their eggs and protect them

5. from _____.

C. Antonyms

Pick the word that means the opposite or near opposite of the word provided.

1.	**nascent**	initial	emerging	incipient	moribund	beginning
2.	**naysayer**	denier	pessimist	apologist	dissenter	cynic
3.	**rumour**	gossip	fact	tale	allegation	claim
4.	**obdurate**	stubborn	rigid	inexorable	inflexible	amenable
5.	**dishevelled**	untidy	rumpled	groomed	tousled	wild
6.	**poltergeist**	ghost	spirit	being	phantom	apparition
7.	**prosaic**	interesting	dull	boring	tedious	ordinary

D. Missing words

Choose the best word to complete the sentences.

A black hole is seen in space where gravitational pull is (1) _____ (extremely, weakly, never) strong. Black holes do not allow light to pass through, (2) _____ (hence, presently, because), black holes are invisible. They are unable to go around solid objects such as planets, moons and stars, (3) _____ (compatible, contrary, same) to popular belief. Most of the black holes (4) _____ (finished, grew, originated) from a large star dying after an explosion. Black holes cannot be observed via telescopes, instead, scientists (5) _____ (oppose, infer, misunderstood) their presence by detecting their effect on other matters nearby.

E. Odd one out

Four of the words in each list are linked. Mark the word that is not related to these four.

Example: red   green   ~~stripy~~   blue   yellow

1.	marigold	hibiscus	lotus	jasmine	rose
2.	chalk	blackboard	desk	bed	eraser
3.	August	July	December	January	June
4.	grandfather	mother	father	nephew	grandmother
5.	father	mother	friend	brother	sister

F. Idioms

Match each idiom to its meaning.

1.	**There is method in my madness**	a. The person you have just been talking about suddenly arrives
2.	**Speak of the devil**	b. To start again after an idea or project has been rejected
3.	**Back to the drawing board**	c. Being angry or overwhelmed by what is happening in the moment
4.	**In the heat of the moment**	d. To deceive someone in order to gain advantage
5.	**Pull wool over other people's eyes**	e. An action that is done in an unorthodox way but with a rational purpose.

Set 21

A. Synonyms

Select the word that most closely matches the meaning of the word provided.

1.	**dismal**	dreary	bright	festive	blithe	glad
2.	**tractable**	stubborn	disobedient	headstrong	compliant	adamant
3.	**promontory**	bay	valley	headland	stream	desert
4.	**forbearing**	clement	pressing	impatient	urgent	petulant
5.	**feign**	real	actual	factual	pretend	visible
6.	**flamboyant**	flashy	modest	plain	prudent	calm
7.	**flora**	animal	fauna	creature	beast	flowers
8.	**frivolous**	solemn	giddy	serious	sensible	thoughtful

B. Fill in the blanks

Fill in the blanks from the words in the table below. There are two extra words you do not need.

industry	supply	stunning	measures	source	power	reservoir

1. Lake Kariba is the largest man-made lake in Africa. It _____ 226 km long and

2. 40 km wide. Lake Kariba serves as a/an _____ in order to store water and provide

3. electric _____ to Zambia and Zimbabwe. A lot of fish species are found in

4. the lake providing a thriving commercial fishing _____ in the area.

5. Lake Kariba is also renowned for its _____ sunsets and spectacular views, attracting

    a lot of tourists.

C. Antonyms

Pick the word that means the opposite or near opposite of the word provided.

1.	**latent**	dormant	concealed	active	hidden	inert
2.	**nonchalant**	cool	indifferent	apathetic	anxious	insouciant
3.	**condone**	forbid	forgive	pardon	overlook	excuse
4.	**rudimentary**	underdeveloped	basic	primitive	vestigial	sophisticated
5.	**confound**	bewilder	enlighten	baffle	puzzle	mystify
6.	**dupe**	gull	trick	fool	deceive	acquaint
7.	**senescent**	aging	juvenile	decrepit	elderly	senior
8.	**malleable**	pliable	flexible	compliant	firm	supple

D. Missing letters

Fill in the missing letters to complete the words in the boxes below.

1. The Tyrannosaurus Rex (T Rex) was the largest [b | _ | p | _ | d | a | _] carnivore that ever lived, around 68 million years ago. They were among the most

2. [_ | e | a | _ | s | _ | m | e | _] and aggressive dinosaurs. They were 20 feet tall,

3. 40 feet long and [w | _ | i | _ | g | _ | e | _] 7 tons. The largest fossil of

4. T-Rex found was female and was [n | _ | m | e | _] Sue, after its discoverer, Sue

5. Hendrickson. Many other T Rex fossils have been [f | _ | u | _ | d] in Texas, Utah, Wyoming, Canada and Mongolia.

E. Homophones and homographs

Homophones are two or more words having the same pronunciation but different spellings and meanings. Homographs are words which have the same spelling but different meanings.

From the list below, fill in the blanks. (The first one has been done for you).

| gait | gate | spare | desert | box | dessert |

1. An opening in a wall or fence   _____gate_____
2. An area of dry land with little to no rainfall and sparse vegetation   __desert__
3. A sweet dish served at the end of a meal   __dessert__
4. To fight using fists   __box__
5. Describing a slim person   __spare__
6. A manner of walking or moving on foot   __gait__
7. A rigid rectangular container with or without a cover   __box__
8. A replacement part e.g. for a car   __spare__

Set 22

A. Synonyms

Select the word that most closely matches the meaning of the word provided.

1.	**promenade**	run	scurry	parade	bolt	scamper
2.	**ambiguous**	indefinite	explicit	lucid	obvious	certain
3.	**homogeneous**	diverse	uniform	miscellaneous	varied	assorted
4.	**contentious**	peaceful	appeasing	agreed	combative	amicable
5.	**metamorphosis**	steady	constant	transformation	stagnant	stable
6.	**inaugural**	final	ultimate	advanced	terminal	first
7.	**vicarious**	surrogate	primary	first hand	direct	Immediate

B. Fill in the blanks

Fill in the blanks from the words in the table below. There are two extra words you do not need.

nocturnal	wholly	trafficked	slightly	elusive	curl	extinct

1. Pangolins are mammals _____ covered in scales which they use to protect

2. themselves from predators. Pangolins are very shy, _____ and secretive

3. mammals. If threatened, Pangolins _____ themselves into a tight ball in

4. order to defend themselves. Pangolins are _____ animals, active at night, and feed on ants and termites. Hunting Pangolins is illegal but they are the most

5. _____ mammals by criminals as their scales and blood are used in traditional Chinese medicine and their meat makes a high-end delicacy in China.

C. Antonyms

Pick the word that means the opposite or near opposite of the word provided.

1.	**pompous**	arrogant	grandiose	submissive	haughty	inflated
2.	**unfathomable**	infinite	obvious	obscure	unintelligible	incomprehensible
3.	**precipitous**	steep	sudden	slight	dramatic	sharp
4.	**retentive**	forgetful	tenacious	mindful	retaining	clinging
5.	**auxiliary**	accessory	secondary	adjunct	fundamental	supplementary
6.	**frenetic**	delirious	balanced	furious	rabid	overwrought
7.	**atrocious**	awful	appalling	terrible	wicked	excellent

D. Missing words

Choose the best word to complete the sentences.

There is a (1) _____ (species, specie, type) called the Blue Dragon which belongs to the family of sea slugs. They have a gas-filled stomach which allows them to (2) _____ (sink, float, dive) upside-down in warm waters. These Blue Dragons prey on small poisonous jellyfish with their strong jaws and (3) _____ (rows, columns, groups) of teeth. Blue dragons are dangerous to humans because they wash up on beaches and they have the ability to (4) _____ (concentrate, dissolve, disappear) the venom they get from their food. Picking up these blue dragons or having (5) _____ (transportation, contact, played) with them may cause a painful sting.

E. Odd one out

Four of the words in each list are linked. Mark the word that is not related to these four.

Example: red   green   ~~stripy~~   blue   yellow

1.	radish	carrot	eggplant	potato	ginger
2.	sentence	word	alphabet	page	paragraph
3.	cake	salad	bread	biscuit	pastry
4.	bird	airplane	kite	helicopter	lizard
5.	Japan	Finland	Laos	Cambodia	Vietnam

F. Idioms

Match each idiom to its meaning.

1. **Hit the sack**   a. Do or say something exactly right or accurate

2. **Off one's rocker**   b. Go to bed and sleep

3. **Hit the nail on the head**   c. Someone who is knowledgeable and competent

4. **Don't judge a book by its cover** d. Be crazy, demented, out of one's mind

5. **On the ball**   e. Do not base your opinion on something based on its superficial qualities

Set 23

A. Synonyms

Select the word that most closely matches the meaning of the word provided.

1.	**abscond**	abide	escape	dwell	endure	remain
2.	**tactful**	inconsiderate	blunt	thoughtless	judicious	silly
3.	**discreet**	foolish	prudent	reckless	idiotic	contemptuous
4.	**mediocre**	substandard	superb	superior	exceptional	top
5.	**whim**	caprice	plan	reality	permanence	fact
6.	**animosity**	affection	charity	enmity	compassion	empathy
7.	**doting**	canny	amorous	despised	apathetic	disapproving
8.	**detrimental**	benign	favourable	convenient	advantageous	pernicious

B. Fill in the blanks

Fill in the blanks from the words in the table below. There are two extra words you do not need.

volumes	houses	purchased	bookshelves	turn	catalogues	tear

1. The Library of Congress is the biggest library in the world and holds 838 miles of _____

2. with more than 167 million items. Its first major collection was _____ during

3. 1815 after British troops burned down the library and destroyed almost 3,000 _____

4. during a war in 1814. The Library of Congress _____ the smallest book in the

5. world which is entitled, 'Old King Cole'. You can _____ its pages with a needle.

C. Antonyms

Pick the word that means the opposite or near opposite of the word provided.

1.	**deplorable**	grievous	commendable	wretched	woeful	distressing
2.	**alfresco**	indoor	exterior	outdoor	open air	atmospheric
3.	**loot**	ransack	despoil	pillage	give	plunder
4.	**combustible**	inert	burning	flammable	explosive	dangerous
5.	**iniquitous**	immoral	evil	virtuous	depraved	corrupt
6.	**posterity**	descendant	predecessor	offspring	brood	progeny
7.	**imminent**	impending	approaching	close	coming	distant
8.	**tantalizing**	alluring	tempting	fascinating	repulsive	captivating

D. Missing letters

Fill in the missing letters to complete the words in the boxes below.

1. Most snakes creep and ☐ | l | ☐ | t | h | ☐ | r ☐ in order to move, but

2. researchers have recently ☐ | i | ☐ | c | ☐ | v | ☐ | e | d ☐ a snake

with four, small legs. Just like other snakes, they have a good

3. | v | e | ☐ | ☐ | e | ☐ | r | ☐ | l | structure to strangle their prey.

4. However, scientists have been taking part in a ☐ d | ☐ | b | ☐ | ☐ | e | ☐ about

5. whether they are true snakes or aquatic lizards. They are also digging deeper to find out if snakes | e | ☐ | o | l | ☐ | ☐ | d | ☐ from lizards at some point in the past.

E. Homophones and homographs

Homophones are two or more words having the same pronunciation but different spellings and meanings. Homographs are words which have the same spelling but different meanings.

From the list below, fill in the blanks. (The first one has been done for you).

| peal | peel | buckle | hatch | mind |

1. To become aware, to regard with attention _____mind_____
2. To strip off an outer layer _____
3. A clasp used for fastening two loose ends seen in a belt or strap _____
4. The part of the human body that thinks, reasons, feels or remembers _____
5. A small door or opening _____
6. The loud ringing of bells _____
7. Bend and give way under pressure or strain _____
8. To emerge from an egg, cocoon or a structure that surrounds a young one _____

Set 24

A. Synonyms

Select the word that most closely matches the meaning of the word provided.

1.	**atheist**	pagan	non-believing	religious	devout	monotheistic
2.	**deity**	human	mortal	divine	fleshly	earthborn
3.	**belligerent**	pacifist	hostile	friendly	amicable	affable
4.	**fallow**	active	developed	fertile	barren	cultivated
5.	**bleak**	dismal	sunny	encouraging	pleasant	festive
5.	**formidable**	feeble	weak	easy	simple	colossal
6.	**accolade**	reprimand	punishment	applause	demerit	insult

B. Fill in the blanks

Fill in the blanks from the words in the table below.

consists	recent	weird	tails	incisors	inhabitant	hind

1. Another _____ animal discovered recently is a pig-nosed rat with vampire teeth.

2. This odd-looking creature is a/an _____ of Indonesia. What makes them stand

3. out from all other species of rats are their extremely long _____ which are used for

4. cutting. Despite this they have weak jaws, so their diet _____ only of soft food

5. such as beetle larva and earthworms. They also have very large ears and long _____ legs

   which are used for hopping.

C. Antonyms

Pick the word that means the opposite or near opposite of the word provided.

1.	**reluctant**	hesitant	loath	unwilling	wary	eager
2.	**outlaw**	legalize	prohibit	criminal	ban	interdict
3.	**emigrate**	migrate	remain	move	relocate	leave
4.	**incite**	provoke	stimulate	instigate	deter	motivate
5.	**digress**	deviate	concentrate	diverge	wander	divagate
6.	**serene**	tranquil	peaceful	frantic	placid	composed
7.	**disdain**	contempt	sympathy	scorn	disregard	spurn

D. Missing words

Choose the best word to complete the sentences.

George Washington was an American (1) _____ (general, police officer, doctor) and commander in chief of the colonel armies. He subsequently (2) _____ (becomes, became, become) the first president of the United States. Washington's father, Augustine Washington, had gone to (3) _____ (market, park, school) in England, tasted seafaring life and then emigrated to the American colonies where he (4) _____ (settled, burrowed, dug) down to manage his growing Virginia estates. Washington came from a distinguished (5) _____ (paternal, geologic, fossil) lineage as an early forebear was described as a "gentleman".

E. Odd one out

Four of the words in each list are linked. Mark the word that is not related to these four.

Example: red   green   ~~stripy~~   blue   yellow

1.	Saturn	Uranus	Sun	Earth	Mercury
2.	cork	stone	paper	feather	foam
3.	grapes	mangoes	lychees	lettuces	apples
4.	harbour	coast	island	oasis	reef
5.	Mandarin	English	Europe	Nihongo	German

F. Idioms

Match each idiom to its meaning.

1.	**Bite off more than you can chew**	a. An event or a show that has come to an end; someone has left the place
2.	**Elvis has left the building**	b. To take on a task that is way too big or too difficult
3.	**A dime a dozen**	c. To have a neutral opinion before all the facts are disclosed
4.	**Give the benefit of the doubt**	d. An event or situation that is unfortunate at first but then yields a positive result
5.	**A blessing in disguise**	e. Something common that has little to no value

Set 25

A. Synonyms

Select the word that most closely matches the meaning of the word provided.

1.	**antagonist**	supporter	adversary	buddy	sidekick	ally
2.	**ingenious**	shrewd	ignorant	incompetent	awkward	dull
3.	**ingenuous**	crafty	deceitful	candid	phony	sly
4.	**solace**	distress	anguish	agony	comfort	affliction
5.	**torrid**	fiery	frigid	cold	chilly	cool
6.	**fickle**	constant	volatile	reliable	steadfast	persistent
7.	**recoil**	remain	advance	approach	confront	ricochet
8.	**slovenly**	spruce	dapper	meticulous	unkempt	orderly

B. Fill in the blanks

Fill in the blanks from the words in the table below. There are two extra words you do not need.

pseudonym	draft	father	scientist	elegance	diplomat	consistency

1. Benjamin Franklin, who also used the _____ Richard Saunders, was an

2. American author, inventor, _____ and diplomat. As one of the Founding

3. Fathers, he helped _____ the Declaration of Independence and represented

4. the United States as a _____ during the American Revolution. In addition, he

5. made important contributions in science, and is remembered for his _____ in

   writing.

C. Antonyms

Pick the word that means the opposite or near opposite of the word provided.

1.	**onerous**	effortless	arduous	difficult	oppressive	harsh
2.	**gaunt**	scrawny	haggard	thin	plump	lean
3.	**implausible**	improbable	feasible	farfetched	dubious	unlikely
4.	**emaciated**	bony	spare	obese	wasted	lank
5.	**repugnant**	offensive	revolting	loathsome	repulsive	appealing
6.	**undulation**	oscillation	ripple	flatness	pulsation	vibration
7.	**pertinacious**	amenable	stubborn	tenacious	obstinate	resolute
8.	**consensus**	dissension	unity	concurrence	accord	concord

D. Missing letters

Fill in the missing letters to complete the words in the boxes below.

1. Sloths are very [_ | r | _ | w | _ | _ | y] tree dwelling animals which can sleep

2. up to 20 hours per day. They [r | e | _ | _ | _ | b | l | _] monkeys but are true

3. relatives of armadillos. They spend a lot of time [h | _ | n | _ | g | _ | _ | g]

4. upside down in trees. They are really [s | _ | u | g | _ | i | _ | h] and have

5. given their name to the condition of being lazy. Because of this, they make a great

5. [_ | o | m | _ | _ | n] for algae and fungi.

E. Homophones and homographs

Homophones are two or more words having the same pronunciation but different spellings and meanings. Homographs are words which have the same spelling but different meanings.

From the list below, fill in the blanks. (The first one has been done for you).

| hanger | hangar | refrain | charge | mole |

1. To impose a financial burden on — _____charge_____
2. A spy working in an organization — _____
3. A building where aircraft are stored or repaired — _____
4. To rush forward violently; to run — _____
5. To stop yourself from doing something — _____
6. A pigmented spot, mark, or a raised lesion on the human body — _____
7. A device on which a garment is hung — _____
8. A phrase or verse that is repeated regularly in a poem or song — _____

Set 26

A. Synonyms

Select the word that most closely matches the meaning of the word provided.

1. **decorum**   vulgarity   propriety   impropriety   rudeness   crudity
2. **benevolent** charitable   malevolent   hateful   merciless   cruel
3. **benign**   hostile   malignant   harsh   amiable   adverse
4. **pious**   devout   irreverent   atheist   blasphemous sinful
5. **jostle**   pull   tug   shove   ignore   leave
6. **averse**   positive   inclined   greedy   hesitant   desirous
7. **revelry**   sobriety   gaiety   unhappiness   mourning   abstinence

B. Fill in the blanks

Fill in the blanks from the words in the table below.

composed	fifth	sixth	mythology	discovered	blue	massive

1. Jupiter, the _____ planet from the Sun, is the largest planet in the solar system.
2. It was named after the king of the gods in Roman _____. In 1610, Galileo
3. _____ that Jupiter has four moons, now named as Galilean moons. Its
4. atmosphere is similar to that of the sun, _____ mostly of hydrogen and
5. helium. Jupiter is said to be so _____ that it could hold up to 1,300 Earths.

C. Antonyms

Pick the word that means the opposite or near opposite of the word provided.

1.	**beckoning**	inviting	summoning	repelling	tempting	waving
2.	**char**	extinguish	scorch	burn	sear	roast
3.	**din**	ruckus	commotion	clamour	stillness	uproar
4.	**derogatory**	insulting	depreciative	flattering	abusive	offensive
5.	**gregarious**	sociable	outgoing	congenial	hospitable	introvert
6.	**innocuous**	pernicious	innocent	jejune	naïve	safe
7.	**intangible**	impalpable	airy	concrete	elusive	ethereal

D. Missing words

Choose the best word to complete the sentences.

Angel Falls in Venezuela is the world's highest (1) _____ (uninterrupted, interrupted, interjected) waterfall. The waterfall is named after Jimmie Angel, the first American (2) _____ (seaman, aviator, engineer) who flew over the falls. Angel Falls is best seen (3) _____ (behind, beyond, between) the months of May and November. Tourists are advised to avoid visiting the falls from December to April as rainfall is (4) _____ (scarce, abundant, bountiful) and the falls dry up. Angel Falls has (5) _____ (scared, frightened, inspired) several movies such as "Up", where it was called the Paradise Falls.

E. Odd one out

Four of the words in each list are linked. Mark the word that is not related to these four.

Example: red   green   ~~stripy~~   blue   yellow

1.	stone	metal	rock	oxygen	glass
2.	book	laptop	wallet	bag	ball pen
3.	carpenter	barber	bricklayer	electrician	plumber
4.	staircase	ladder	bridge	elevator	escalator
5.	carbon	iron	glass	wood	silicon

F. Idioms

Match each idiom to its meaning.

1. **Bite the bullet**   a. In order to achieve something, you have to go through some unpleasant things
2. **Well begun is half done**   b. Try to do something advanced before you have learned the basics of the subject
3. **Run before you can walk**   c. To finally accept an unpleasant or difficult situation
4. **As easy as falling off a log**   d. Something is really simple and harmless
5. **You can't make an omelette without breaking some eggs**   e. Making a good start in doing a task will make it easier to finish it

Set 27

A. Synonyms

Select the word that most closely matches the meaning of the word provided.

1. **nurseryman**   gardener   doctor   engineer   architect   teacher
2. **obscure**   visible   famous   hazy   transparent   distinct
3. **ostentatious**   gaudy   reserved   plain   humble   modest
4. **painstaking**   thoughtless   meticulous   disorganised   careless   casual
5. **perplexing**   clear   straightforward   logical   confusing   precise
6. **deduce**   confound   know   surmise   ascertain   prove
7. **placid**   boisterous   tranquil   upset   violent   agitated
8. **precarious**   safe   strong   certain   firm   perilous

B. Fill in the blanks

Fill in the blanks from the words in the table below. There are two extra words you do not need.

fossil	extinct	canine	mammal	build	robust	scavengers

1. An Amphicyon was a pre-historic _____ omnivore which lived 30 million years
2. ago. They are known as "bear dogs" because of their _____ skeletal structure,
3. they looked more like a modern bear than a dog. Amphicyons were _____ and
4. would eat anything that they could find, even dead animals. Because of their large _____
5. it is believed that they became _____ because of their slow pace.

C. Antonyms

Pick the word that means the opposite or near opposite of the word provided.

1.	**prejudice**	bias	partiality	equity	bigotry	influence
2.	**capacious**	spacious	ample	expansive	restricted	voluminous
3.	**quell**	quash	overpower	subdue	incite	suppress
4.	**garble**	falsify	decipher	misrepresent	pervert	confuse
5.	**precedence**	inferiority	antecedence	superiority	supremacy	priority
6.	**raiment**	undress	garb	apparel	clothing	attire
7.	**acrimonious**	caustic	bitter	pleasant	sarcastic	acerbic
8.	**subterfuge**	artifice	ploy	deception	trick	honesty

D. Missing letters

Fill in the missing letters to complete the words in the boxes below.

1. Pterodactyls are [_ | x | _ | _ | n | c | _] dinosaurs which lived during the late

2. Jurassic period. They were winged [r | _ | p | _ | i | _ | s] but had no feathers.

3. Palaeontologists believe they were [_ | q | _ | a | t | _ | c] animals and

their wings served as flippers. They also had strong muscles which they used to walk as

4. [q | _ | a | d | _ | p | d | _] Similar to Vampire Bats. One interesting

5. is that all the fossils discovered so far were [j | _ | v | _ | _ | i | l | _] and the adult form remains a mystery.

E. Homophones and homographs

Homophones are two or more words having the same pronunciation but different spellings and meanings. Homographs are words which have the same spelling but different meanings.

From the list below, fill in the blanks. (The first one has been done for you).

| dough | doe | fuse | coach | discount |

1. A safety device that breaks an electric circuit if the current exceeds a safe level _____fuse_____

2. A vehicle designed to be used for long distance transportation _____

3. A mixture that consists of flour and a liquid used for baking pastries _____

4. To sell a product at a reduced price _____

5. To blend or join two or more different elements together _____

6. A female deer _____

7. To disregard something or someone as untrustworthy _____

8. One who instructs or trains _____

Set 28

A. Synonyms

Select the word that most closely matches the meaning of the word provided.

1. **darkness**   day   night   morning   dawn   sunrise
2. **equilibrium**   imbalance   stability   inequality   shakiness   vibration
3. **egocentric**   conceited   selfless   modest   considerate   altruistic
4. **liable**   exempt   unaccountable   insured   immune   accountable
5. **conferrer**   retriever   donor   antagonist   denier   host
6. **exonerate**   condemn   punish   incriminate   acquit   convict
7. **incriminate**   exonerate   exculpate   implicate   absolve   vindicate

B. Fill in the blanks

Fill in the blanks from the words in the table below.

capability	underwater	coastal	source	warm	ivory	pollution

1. Narwhals, the unicorns of the sea, are found in the _____ waters of the Arctic
2. Ocean. They have a/an _____ tooth that grows right through their upper lip. Many
3. people hunt narwhals for their skin because it is an important _____ of Vitamin C.
4. The Narwhal tusk has a sensory _____ and has 10 million nerves inside.
5. However, noise pollution becomes a threat for Narwhals as more _____ noise interferes with their communication.

C. Antonyms

Pick the word that means the opposite or near opposite of the word provided.

1.	**astound**	confirm	astonish	dumbfound	stun	startle
2.	**valour**	bravery	courage	timidity	heroism	manliness
3.	**prickly**	barbed	blunt	sharp	spiky	bristly
4.	**wily**	cunning	shrewd	clever	ingenuous	scheming
5.	**swindle**	cheat	defraud	dupe	deceive	give
6.	**abyss**	gulf	utopia	void	chasm	gorge
7.	**incongruous**	contradictory	harmonious	absurd	improper	discordant

D. Missing words

Choose the best word to complete the sentences.

Venus is the (1) _____ (first, second, third) planet from the Sun and was named after the Roman goddess of love and beauty. This is the only planet named after a female goddess because it (2) _____ (shines, shine, shone) the brightest among all the planets. Venus and Earth are often called twins because of their (3) _____ (similar, different, divergent) size, mass and composition. However, it is the hottest planet in the solar system because it (4) _____ (consists, differ, negate) of carbon dioxide and clouds of sulphuric acid.

Water on Venus (5) _____ (evaporates, forms, appears) quickly because of the scorching heat its atmosphere produces.

E. Odd one out

Four of the words in each list are linked. Mark the word that is not related to these four.

Example: red   green   ~~stripy~~   blue   yellow

1.	slippers	loafers	boots	jeans	sandals
2.	shirt	cardigan	socks	sweater	jacket
3.	gram	kilogram	pound	ton	centimetre
4.	flood	typhoon	explosion	earthquake	tsunami
5.	minute	hour	mile	second	millisecond

F. Idioms

Match each idiom to its meaning.

1. **That ship has sailed**   a. An opportunity or situation that cannot be changed anymore

2. **There are clouds on the horizon**   b. You can give someone advice, but you can never force them to do something they do not want to do

3. **The pot calling the kettle black**   c. A sign or omen that a problem will happen in the future

4. **When it rains it pours**   d. Accusing someone of something that you are also guilty of, hypocrisy

5. **You can lead a horse to water, but you can't make it drink**   e. When something bad happens, something else as bad or worse follows

Set 29

A. Synonyms

Select the word that most closely matches the meaning of the word provided.

1.	**anecdote**	novel	parable	ode	thesis	lyric
2.	**blatant**	strident	subtle	concealed	shameful	invisible
3.	**fertile**	infertile	barren	poor	cultivable	impoverished
4.	**ashen**	rosy	pale	colourful	blooming	tanned
5.	**blight**	blessing	health	boon	affliction	benefit
6.	**tempest**	typhoon	calm	breeze	air	sough
7.	**glower**	smile	grin	cheer	grimace	brighten
8.	**flimsy**	durable	hard	tough	solid	insubstantial

B. Fill in the blanks

Fill in the blanks from the words in the table below. There are two extra words you do not need.

orbit	equator	considered	gathered	surface	discovered	moon

1. In 1930, Pluto was discovered and _____ to be the solar system's ninth planet.

2. Pluto is known to _____ the sun 40 times as far as the Earth. The

3. _____ of Pluto is tannish-red in colour. There is also a bright area on its surface which is

4. shaped like a heart near its _____. However, in 2015, additional data was

5. _____ from Pluto and since then, it has been reclassified as a dwarf planet.

C. Antonyms

Pick the word that means the opposite or near opposite of the word provided.

1.	**stench**	reek	fug	stink	malodour	essence
2.	**gangling**	scrawny	brawny	gaunt	slender	emaciated
3.	**euphoric**	blissful	intoxicated	despondent	rapturous	elated
4.	**contrive**	improvise	demolish	concoct	frame	fabricate
5.	**skittish**	audacious	nervous	restless	timid	jumpy
6.	**superfluous**	redundant	indispensable	spare	needless	unnecessary
7.	**nippy**	lukewarm	cold	frosty	biting	brisk
8.	**callous**	hard	insensible	sensitive	aloof	ruthless

D. Missing letters

Fill in the missing letters to complete the words in the boxes below.

1. The Philippine Tarsier or Tarsus Syrichta is a very | | e | c | u | | a | r |

2. | | o | c | | u | | n | a | l | animal. This means they are more active

3. at night. They live on the roots and trunks of | t | | | e | s | such as bamboo.

4. Tarsiers are known to have | e | | o | r | | o | u | | eyes which are bigger

5. than their brains. The tarsier is the smallest carnivorous | p | | | m | | t | in the world.

E. Homophones and homographs

Homophones are two or more words having the same pronunciation but different spellings and meanings. Homographs are words which have the same spelling but different meanings.

From the list below, fill in the blanks. (The first one has been done for you).

air	heir	defect	date	company

1. One who is entitled to inherit a property   _____heir_____

2. A romantic meeting with someone   _____

3. A group of persons or assembly   _____

4. To forsake a cause, political party, or nation because of a change in ideology   _____

5. A business organization that makes, buys, or sells goods or provides services in exchange for money   _____

6. The particular day on which an event occurs   _____

7. An imperfection that impairs worth or utility   _____

8. The mixture of colourless, odourless, tasteless gases that surrounds the earth   _____

Set 30

A. Synonyms

Select the word that most closely matches the meaning of the word.

1.	**seep**	permeate	surge	cascade	downpour	flood
2.	**wallop**	stroke	release	pummel	caress	hold
3.	**scuffle**	agreement	affray	deal	accord	connection
4.	**blithe**	blue	morose	anguished	buoyant	black
5.	**pensive**	thoughtless	ignorant	wistful	shallow	carefree
6.	**acrid**	honeyed	luscious	cordial	savoury	pungent
7.	**scruple**	ignorance	conviction	negligence	hesitation	certainty

B. Fill in the blanks

Fill in the blanks from the words in the table below. There are two extra words you do not need.

exclusively	aquatic	forests	freshwater	derived	resemble	vegetarian

1. The weirdest turtle is found in the _____ rivers of South America. They easily

2. blend in leaf litter along the river banks because their heads _____ a leaf and their

3. shells look like the bark of a tree. They are strictly _____ animals and prefer to

4. stand in shallow waters. Their name, Mata Mata, is _____ from the Spanish term

5. which means, "kill, kill". These turtles are carnivorous species which feed _____ on

   live fish.

C. Antonyms

Pick the word that means the opposite or near opposite of the word provided.

1.	**reverie**	daydream	reality	fantasy	trance	absorption
2.	**connive**	scheme	machinate	intrigue	collude	preclude
3.	**temerity**	daring	presumption	boldness	caution	overconfidence
4.	**censure**	endorse	rebuke	scold	denounce	condemn
5.	**puny**	gargantuan	feeble	weak	frail	petty
6.	**bygone**	ancient	archaic	forthcoming	vintage	departed
7.	**supple**	pliable	limber	lithe	flexible	stiff

D. Missing words

Choose the best word to complete the sentences.

A Pacu fish is a/an (1) _____ (carnivore, herbivore, omnivore) which feeds on both plants and animals. They are related to piranhas, however, what makes them (2) _____ (unique, similar, alike) is that they possess teeth similar to humans. Pacu fish are popular pets as they develop (3) _____ (personalities, teeth, feet) over time and can recognise their owners. But Pacu fish are difficult to look after. They are extremely powerful and they can (4) _____ (build, jump, assemble) out of their aquariums when excited. Pacu fish are also very (5) _____ (aggressive, shy, timid) when frightened and they have an extremely powerful bite which may injure their owners.

E. Odd one out

Four of the words in each list are linked. Mark the word that is not related to these four.

Example: red   green   ~~stripy~~   blue   yellow

1.	pen	calculator	pencil	ink	chalk
2.	eagle	hornbill	condor	crane	ostrich
3.	hydrogen	helium	iodine	oxygen	nitrogen
4.	pineapple	watermelon	orange	banana	lemon
5.	diameter	radius	chord	angle	circumference

F. Idioms

Match each idiom to its meaning.

1. **Time is money**
2. **People who live in glass houses shouldn't throw stones**
3. **Shape up or ship out**
4. **Through thick and thin**
5. **Waste not, want not**

a. Either improve your performance at work or leave

b. Use your resources wisely in order to have enough

c. Work as quickly as possible

d. Do not criticize others for the mistakes or faults that you are also guilty of

e. Through good and bad times

Set 31

A. Synonyms

Select the word that most closely matches the meaning of the word provided.

1.	**crass**	refined	vulgar	sensitive	considerate	beautiful
2.	**apportion**	keep	hold	retain	allot	accumulate
3.	**shun**	accept	embrace	elude	abide	intervene
4.	**bewilderment**	perplexity	certainty	clarity	assurance	scrutiny
5.	**strut**	hobble	parade	stroll	conceal	skip
6.	**maim**	mend	heal	mutilate	convalesce	repair
7.	**provisional**	interim	permanent	definite	settled	decisive
8.	**discretion**	paranoia	carelessness	indecency	discernment	insanity

B. Fill in the blanks

Fill in the blanks from the words in the table below.

freedom	courage	gift	designer	landmark	inscribed	same

1. The Statue of Liberty is a copper statue which symbolises _____ and

2. democracy. It was given by the people of France as a/an _____ to the United States.

3. The person who designed the Statue of Liberty, is the _____ person who built the Eiffel tower, Gustave Eiffel. The Statue of Liberty holds a torch above her head and the date of

4. independence is _____ in her left hand. In 1984, UNESCO designated this

5. _____ as a World Heritage Site.

C. Antonyms

Pick the word that means the opposite or near opposite of the word provided.

1.	**drab**	dreary	boring	delightful	dark	gloomy
2.	**anthology**	single	collection	compendium	album	compilation
3.	**abominable**	alluring	repulsive	loathsome	disgusting	horrid
4.	**indignant**	annoyed	resentful	pleased	irritated	disturbed
5.	**autonomous**	independent	free	subordinate	sovereign	discrete
6.	**auspicious**	propitious	ominous	opportune	fortunate	promising
7.	**brazen**	meek	bold	insolent	shameless	impertinent
8.	**venal**	greedy	mercenary	corrupt	sordid	ethical

D. Missing letters

Fill in the missing letters to complete the words in the boxes below.

1. Okapis are known as forest giraffes. They | b | | a | | the striped markings of a zebra

2. but are closely related to giraffes. They are reddish brown in | | o | l | | u | |

and have stripes on their legs and ankles. Okapis, are not as tall as giraffes. They have

3. | s | | o | | | e | | legs and necks than giraffes. Okapis eat only leaves,

4. grass, fruits and fungi, so they are | h | | | b | | v | | | e | s |

5. Okapis are now considered to be | e | | d | | | g | | r | e | |

because humans hunt them for their skin and meat.

E. Homophones and homographs

Homophones are two or more words having the same pronunciation but different spellings and meanings. Homographs are words which have the same spelling but different meanings.

From the list below, fill in the blanks. (The first one has been done for you).

heal	heel	bar	compact	foot

1. Having a dense structure or parts or units closely packed or joined — _____compact_____

2. A unit of measurement equal to 1/3 yard (0.3048 meter) or 12 inches — _____

3. To recover from an injury or disease — _____

4. A straight, rigid piece made of metal or wood that is used as a fastener or mechanical part — _____

5. The part of the body on which an animal or person stands and moves — _____

6. The rounded portion of the human foot behind the ankle and behind the arch — _____

7. Something that obstructs or prevents passage, progress, or action — _____

8. An agreement or covenant between two or more parties — _____

Set 32

A. Synonyms

Select the word that most closely matches the meaning of the word provided.

1.	**augment**	abridge	diminish	expand	abate	deplete
2.	**asylum**	sanctuary	threat	danger	eradication	trouble
3.	**betrothal**	divorce	leave	separate	detach	engagement
4.	**scrumptious**	foul	luscious	tasteless	bland	dreadful
5.	**pragmatic**	impractical	idealistic	romantic	reasonable	naive
6.	**exhilaration**	delight	upset	worry	grief	blues
7.	**venial**	tolerable	abominable	unforgivable	unacceptable	devastating

B. Fill in the blanks

Fill in the blanks from the words in the table below.

limbs	confused	scientific	unique	powerful	angle	chamber

1. An Aaxolotl is a/an _____ salamander than can walk through water. The Axolotl

2. should not be _____ with a fish, because it is an amphibian. Unlike reptiles and

3. humans, axolotls have a three _____ heart. Axolotls are widely used

4. as laboratory animals for _____ studies. This may be due to the fact that

5. axolotls are capable of re-growing their lost _____.

C. Antonyms

Pick the word that means the opposite or near opposite of the word provided.

1.	**hamper**	hinder	expedite	impede	handicap	retard
2.	**profligate**	prudent	libertine	prodigal	wanton	dissolute
3.	**improvident**	lavish	careless	rash	judicious	prodigal
4.	**haggle**	concur	negotiate	barter	bargain	debate
5.	**reverberate**	echo	yield	resonate	rebound	recoil
6.	**venerable**	august	aged	juvenile	noble	esteemed
7.	**forlorn**	jovial	disconsolate	melancholy	gloomy	desolate

D. Missing words

Choose the best word to complete the sentences.

The pyramids of Egypt were built during the time when Egypt was one of the (1) _____ (poorest, busiest, richest) and most powerful civilizations in the world. The pyramids, especially the Great Pyramids of Giza, are some of the most (2) _____ (worst, magnificent, weakest) man-made structures in history. Their massive scale reflects the (3) _____ (unique, common, ordinary) role that the pharaoh, or king, played in ancient Egyptian society. Though pyramids were (4) _____ (destroyed, built, broken) from the beginning of the Old Kingdom to the close of the Ptolemaic period in the fourth (5) _____ (century, decade, year) A.D., the peak period of pyramid building began with the late third dynasty and continued until roughly the sixth dynasty (about 2325 B.C.).

E. Odd one out

Four of the words in each list are linked. Mark the word that is not related to these four.

Example: red   green   ~~stripy~~   blue   yellow

1.	cap	helmet	headband	gloves	hat
2.	school	college	university	nursery	academy
3.	woman	lady	boy	female	girl
4.	river	forest	ocean	lake	sea
5.	wheel	seat	dashboard	windshield	oven

F. Idioms

Match each idiom to its meaning.

1.	**Once bitten, twice shy**	a. In a state of extreme happiness
2.	**Snowed under**	b. You tend to be more cautious when you've been hurt before by a thing or a person
3.	**Run like the wind**	c. Coming from a bad situation to a worse situation
4.	**Out of the frying pan and into the fire**	d. To run very fast
5.	**On cloud nine**	e. To be very busy or overworked

Set 33

A. Synonyms

Select the word that most closely matches the meaning of the word provided.

1.	**congeal**	liquefy	flow	clot	separate	melt
2.	**throttle**	asphyxiate	release	breathe	restore	inhale
3.	**vacillate**	persist	determine	stick	oscillate	remain
4.	**perjure**	attest	lie	certify	prove	proclaim
5.	**ancestor**	successor	follower	contemporary	predecessor	inheritor
6.	**bigot**	liberal	debater	zealot	humanitarian	preserver
7.	**acquit**	vindicate	condemn	accuse	incite	punish
8.	**conflagration**	calm	utopia	peace	shade	holocaust

B. Fill in the blanks

Fill in the blanks from the words in the table below.

source	remnant	natural gas	massive	endorheic	junction	inland

1. The Caspian Sea lies at the _____ of Europe and Asia, bordered by Russia, Iran

2. and Kazakhstan. It is a/an _____ body of water, having characteristics of both sea

3. and lake. It is a/an _____ of the ancient ocean called Tethis which existed 50

4. million years ago. It is a/an _____ basin, which means it does not have any outflow

   via a river towards an ocean. The bed of the Caspian Sea also boasts large reserves of

5. _____ which makes it one of the region's most important resources.

C. Antonyms

Pick the word that means the opposite or near opposite of the word provided.

1.	**demise**	dissolution	resurrection	annihilation	eradication	death
2.	**mundane**	ordinary	average	prosaic	routine	exceptional
3.	**amalgamate**	mix	combine	divide	blend	merge
4.	**perturbed**	distressed	annoyed	flustered	composed	anxious
5.	**pivotal**	marginal	crucial	critical	important	essential
6.	**gratuitous**	unnecessary	complimentary	voluntary	reasonable	free
7.	**versatile**	flexible	limited	adaptable	dexterous	multipurpose
8.	**dexterous**	adroit	deft	expert	clumsy	handy

D. Missing letters

Fill in the missing letters to complete the words in the boxes below.

1. The world's smallest snails have been | u | n | | | r | | h | | d |

2. in China. They were found in | l | | m | | s | t | | | e | rocks in Guangxi

3. province. Their shells are only 0.86 mm long and can fit | | n | | s | | | e |

4. the eye of a needle. Their shells are light grey in | c | | | | | | r |

5. These snails eat | m | i | | r | | o | | g | | | i | s | | s |

such as bacteria and fungi.

E. Homophones and homographs

Homophones are two or more words having the same pronunciation but different spellings and meanings. Homographs are words which have the same spelling but different meanings.

From the list below, fill in the blanks. (The first one has been done for you).

| whack | wax | close | pupil | rock |

1. A child or young person in school   _____pupil_____
2. To strike with a sharp or resounding blow   _____
3. A large mass of stone forming a cliff, promontory, or peak   _____
4. To move something to cover an opening such as a door   _____
5. Black circular part found in the centre of the eye   _____
6. A pliable or liquid composition used in uniting surfaces, or producing a polished surface   _____
7. To draw near   _____
8. Popular music played on instruments that are amplified electronically _____

Set 34

A. Synonyms

Select the word that most closely matches the meaning of the word provided.

1.	**desiccate**	moisten	dehydrate	wet	dampen	soak
2.	**fissure**	closure	barricade	solid	crack	unbroken
3.	**ferment**	turmoil	quiet	ease	relax	calm
4.	**concur**	disagree	object	accord	dispute	differ
5.	**waver**	determine	fluctuate	resolve	continue	persist
6.	**transpire**	vanish	remove	perish	recede	occur
7.	**epoch**	era	timeless	instant	afternoon	decade

B. Fill in the blanks

Fill in the blanks from the words in the table below. There are two extra words you do not need.

palaeontologists	cannibals	kings	ancestors	bizarre	geologists	prehistoric

1. Sea scorpions are _____ creatures that lived 500 million years ago. Sea scorpions

2. are known as the _____ of the sea, because they eat every small creature that

3. they come across. According to _____, sea scorpions can grow taller than a

4. human being. They are a group of arthropods that are said to be the _____ of

   modern lobsters, and crabs. Researchers have described them as the world's first big predator

5. and argue that they are _____ by today's standards.

C. Antonyms

Pick the word that means the opposite or near opposite of the word provided.

1. **alleviate**   relieve   soothe   mitigate   ease   magnify
2. **exacerbate**   aggravate   improve   worsen   intensify   exasperate
3. **petulant**   even tempered   irritable   irascible   cranky   temperamental
4. **retribution**   retaliation   vengeance   revenge   pardon   reprisal
5. **falter**   totter   endure   stammer   vacillate   hobble
6. **calibrate**   adjust   scale   tune   break   measure
7. **transient**   ephemeral   imminent   fleeting   momentary   brief

D. Missing words

Choose the best word to complete the sentences.

Neptune is the (1) _____ (sixth, seventh, eighth) planet away from the Sun and the most distant now that Pluto is no longer regarded as a plant. Neptune is named after the Roman god of the sea because of the (2) _____ (blue, red, brown) colour given off by its atmosphere. (3) _____ (miniature, massive, minute) storms and strong winds are always present on Neptune, one of which is the Great Dark Spot, a permanent storm as big as the Earth. Neptune is called an ice giant planet and it is the (4) _____ (coldest, warmest, scorching) planet in the Solar System. It has 13 moons, and one of them, Triton, is the only moon which orbits Neptune in a (5) _____ (retrograde, clockwise, centigrade) orbit, in other words it moves opposite to the planet's rotation..

E. Odd One Out

Four of the words in each list are linked. Mark the word that is not related to these four.

Example: red   green   ~~stripy~~   blue   yellow

1.	ecstatic	cheerful	grumpy	joyous	excited
2.	pork	chicken	ham	beef	rice
3.	donkey	horse	dinosaur	dragon	dog
4.	goat	cow	horse	wolf	chicken
5.	bus	car	truck	train	lorry

F. Idioms

Match each idiom to its meaning.

1. **Make hay while the sun shines** — a. To look for a solution everywhere; to use all available resources in order to achieve something

2. **Know which way the wind is blowing** — b. A skill learned before which is difficult to forget

3. **To jump on the bandwagon** — c. To take advantage of a good situation

4. **To leave no stone unturned** — d. To understand a changing situation and to be able to anticipate how it is likely to develop

5. **Like riding a bicycle** — e. To follow something successful or popular; to do what everyone else is doing

Set 35

A. Synonyms

Select the word that most closely matches the meaning of the word provided.

1. **fallacy**   reality   delusion   truth   fidelity   fact
2. **ardent**   indifferent   stoic   cool   apathetic   fervent
3. **patently**   inconspicuously   ambiguously   evidently   falsely   covertly
4. **prolific**   fecund   unproductive   sterile   infertile   impotent
5. **hapless**   wretched   lucky   happy   fortunate   golden
6. **prostrate**   upright   erect   raised   recumbent   vertical
7. **delirious**   sane   lucid   demented   coherent   composed
8. **insidious**   guileless   treacherous   honest   frank   sincere

B. Fill in the blanks

Fill in the blanks from the words in the table below. There are two extra words you do not need.

| power | stomp | pouch | cradle | cup | indigenous | balance |

1. Kangaroos are marsupials, _____ to Australia. Marsupials are animals which
2. carry their young ones in a/an _____. Baby kangaroos are called joeys, which the
3. females _____ in their pouches for about 4 to 10 months. Kangaroos have
4. strong tails which give them _____ every time they jump. When facing danger,
5. they _____ their feet on the ground as a defence mechanism.

C. Antonyms

Pick the word that means the opposite or near opposite of the word provided.

1.	**impel**	urge	propel	dissuade	induce	compel
2.	**frolic**	caper	revel	gambol	frisk	slouch
3.	**imperative**	requisite	indispensable	urgent	needless	crucial
4.	**miser**	spendthrift	cheapskate	stingy	selfish	avaricious
5.	**abhor**	relish	loathe	detest	abominate	execrate
6.	**accentuate**	emphasize	accent	abbreviate	stress	punctuate
7.	**acclimatise**	accustom	extemporise	adjust	adapt	habituate
8.	**acquaint**	inform	introduce	notify	conceal	appraise

D. Missing letters

Fill in the missing letters to complete the words in the boxes below.

1. The Atacama Desert, the driest place on Earth, is a | _ | l | a | _ | e | a | _ |

2. in South America. It has not had any significant | r | _ | i | _ | n | _ | a | _ | l | for

3. 400 years. The mountains that surround the desert block | m | _ | i | _ | s | _ | u | _ | _ |

4. depriving it of any water and nutrients. It is the largest | s | _ | _ | u | _ | _ | e |

5. of sodium nitrate, a | c | _ | m | p | _ | u | _ | d | _ | used for fertilizers.

E. Homophones and homographs

Homophones are two or more words having the same pronunciation but different spellings and meanings. Homographs are words which have the same spelling but different meanings.

From the list below, fill in the blanks. (The first one has been done for you).

| some | sum | blunt | left | down |

1. To be in a sad state; unhappy _____down_____
2. The result of adding two or more numbers _____
3. Past tense and past participle of leave _____
4. Having an edge or point that is not sharp _____
5. Unspecified or partial quantity, portion, or number _____
6. Toward or in a lower physical position _____
7. Slow or deficient in feeling; insensitive _____
8. The side of a person toward the west whenever he or she is facing the north; opposite of right _____

Set 36

A. Synonyms

Select the word that most closely matches the meaning of the word provided.

1. **adversary**   ally   assailant   supporter   friend   assistant
2. **allure**   dissuade   discourage   warn   entice   deter
3. **invoice**   debit   bill   credit   voucher   accounts
4. **apathetic**   fervent   zealous   indifferent   ardent   vehement
5. **arbitrary**   circumspect   despotic   rational   democratic   objective
6. **aspire**   descend   plummet   accede   plunge   desire
7. **awry**   amiss   accurate   functioning   correct   even

B. Fill in the blanks

Fill in the blanks from the words in the table below. There are two extra words you do not need.

| surrounding | cured | historian | buried | legend | massive | concrete |

1. Stonehenge is a man-made circle composed of _____ stones. It was built on Salisbury Plain in the UK about 4,000 years ago, with 30 stones in the outer circle

2. _____ five huge inner stones. It has always been a puzzle how these stones were

3. transported, but one _____ claims that a wizard moved the stones from Ireland to England. The purpose of Stonehenge also remains a mystery. One theory is that people were

4. _____ in its grounds and it was used as a cemetery. Other people believe that

5. Stonehenge was a place of healing and anyone brought there was _____ by the stones.

C. Antonyms

Pick the word that means the opposite or near opposite of the word provided.

1.	**berate**	rebuke	scold	applaud	reprimand	chide
2.	**boycott**	support	blacklist	banish	proscribe	ostracize
3.	**charlatan**	swindler	fraudster	impostor	expert	cheat
4.	**clamour**	commotion	silence	uproar	racket	outcry
5.	**commemorate**	memorialize	solemnize	honour	immortalize	dishonour
6.	**conceive**	formulate	create	destroy	devise	contrive
7.	**congregate**	convene	disperse	throng	muster	assemble

D. Missing words

Choose the best word to complete the sentences.

Diwali is a traditional Indian (1) _____ (festival, birthday, rumour) of lights celebrated annually for five days. The word Diwali means, "row of lights" in Sanskrit, the (2) _____ (present, ancient, future) language of India. Diwali is celebrated to (3) _____ (slander, embarrass, honour) the goddess of wealth, Lakshmi. It is said that the lights and lamps during the celebration will (4) _____ (guide, disgruntle, anger) Lakshmi into people's homes, bringing prosperity. People also take this time to enjoy precious moments with friends and family, as well as (5) _____ (trash, decorate, close) and clean their homes.

E. Odd One Out

Four of the words in each list are linked. Mark the word that is not related to these four.

Example: red   green   ~~stripy~~   blue   yellow

1.	France	Tokyo	Thailand	Malaysia	Italy
2.	bottle	water	pencil	spoon	stone
3.	peacock	snake	parrot	ostrich	sparrow
4.	ball	basket	pitch	court	referee
5.	book	television	pen	eraser	paper

F. Idioms

Match each idiom to its meaning.

1. **The darkest hour is just before the dawn**   a. To be impractical, unhelpful or unrealistic about things

2. **A poor workman blames his tools**   b. The worst part always happens just before everything gets better

3. **Have your head in the clouds**   c. You'll make mistakes if you rush through something

4. **Haste makes waste**   d. The one who made the last and final move or decision in a competition, quarrel or feud will be the most successful

5. **He who laughs last laughs loudest**   e. When somebody does a job badly and blames it on somebody or something else instead of taking responsibility for the mistakes

Set 37

A. Synonyms

Select the word that most closely matches the meaning of the word.

1. **contingency** — possibility — certainty — reality — truth — guarantee
2. **counterfeit** — genuine — verifiable — fraudulent — unfeigned — valid
3. **crevice** — closure — bond — cleft — smooth — join
4. **desultory** — methodical — steady — thoughtful — haphazard — consistent
5. **devious** — straightforward — sly — honest — direct — frank
6. **erudite** — fatuous — ignorant — uneducated — ill informed — literate
7. **dissipate** — squander — gather — hoard — conserve — accumulate
8. **dogma** — ambiguity — doubt — ideology — indecision — uncertainty

B. Fill in the blanks

Fill in the blanks from the words in the table below. There are two extra words you do not need.

hibernate	flowers	broad	rarest	born	green	shoots

1. The Giant Panda, one of the world's _____ mammals, lives in the bamboo forests of Sichuan Province, China. These black and white bears almost eat nothing but bamboo

2. _____ and leaves, which account for 99% of their diet. Panda's teeth are

3. _____ and flat, which helps them chomp very thick bamboo shoots and stems.

4. Baby pandas are tiny. They are _____ pink and blind and only open their eyes

5. after 6-8 weeks. They are the only bears who do not _____, instead they head to the lower slopes of the mountains in winter for warmer temperatures and continue eating.

C. Antonyms

Pick the word that means the opposite or near opposite of the word provided.

1.	**dubious**	questionable	suspicious	vague	precarious	definite
2.	**embezzle**	peculate	reimburse	purloin	pilfer	defalcate
3.	**ensuing**	antecedent	subsequent	succeeding	eventual	consequent
4.	**estuary**	creek	inlet	firth	source	delta
5.	**panorama**	view	interior	vista	spectacle	expanse
6.	**reclusive**	solitary	lonely	misanthropic	extrovert	cloistered
7.	**excursion**	journey	outing	expedition	voyage	sedentary
8.	**taciturn**	reserved	outspoken	mute	reticent	aloof

D. Missing letters

Fill in the missing letters to complete the words in the boxes below.

1. The Tasmanian devil is a real f _ i _ t _ animal similar to its

2. cartoon counterpart. They look cute and p _ _ d g _ but they can deliver

3. the most powerful bite in the world. Their main diet is _ a _ r i _ n

4. or dead and decaying flesh. Just like Taz in the cartoon they s _ _ _ n around in

5. circles, howl and shriek when threatened. They are nocturnal animals and spend most of their time in _ o l _ _ w logs or caves.

E. Homophones and homographs

Homophones are two or more words having the same pronunciation but different spellings and meanings. Homographs are words which have the same spelling but different meanings.

From the list below, fill in the blanks. (The first one has been done for you).

| brews | bruise | batter | solution | minor |

1. An injury involving rupture of small blood vessels and discoloration without a break in the overlying skin — bruise

2. A mixture of two or more solid or liquid substances — _____

3. Inferior or lesser in importance, size, or degree — _____

4. Beverages made by steeping, boiling, and fermentation or by infusion and fermentation — _____

5. To beat with successive blows so as to hurt, shatter, or demolish — _____

6. Someone who is not yet old enough to have the rights of an adult — _____

7. An action or process of solving a problem — _____

8. A mixture consisting of flour, egg, and milk or water used in cooking — _____

Set 38

A. Synonyms

Select the word that most closely matches the meaning of the word provided.

1.	**uncouth**	crude	urbane	courteous	cultured	classy
2.	**exuberant**	ebullient	crestfallen	downcast	morose	discouraged
3.	**faction**	unity	conformity	entirety	clique	alliance
4.	**ferocity**	humility	vehemence	clemency	geniality	benevolence
5.	**upheaval**	stagnation	stability	tumult	harmony	peace
6.	**verbose**	succinct	redundant	concise	brief	curt
7.	**frigid**	warm-hearted	torrid	indifferent	ardent	amorous

B. Fill in the blanks

Fill in the blanks from the words in the table below.

planned	piloted	experimenting	invented	sceptical	observed	flap

1. The first airplane was _____ by brothers Orville and Wilbur Wright. They worked

2. for many years _____ and perfecting the design and control of their invention.

3. They studied how birds flew and _____ their wings in order to help

4. them build their very first airplane. The first flight was _____ by Orville Wright

5. and lasted for a mere 59 seconds. However, American experts were _____ about

   the claims of the Wright brothers. They decided to take their airplane to France where people were

   more receptive to their invention.

C. Antonyms

Pick the word that means the opposite or near opposite of the word provided.

1. **predicament**   dilemma   clear cut   pickle   quandary   crisis
2. **gnarled**   knotted   contorted   smooth   wrinkled   warped
3. **grotesque**   hideous   bizarre   repulsive   ludicrous   aesthetic
4. **herald**   harbinger   reflection   precursor   portent   premonition
5. **impertinent**   decent   insolent   impudent   brazen   presumptuous
6. **incantation**   spell   witchcraft   science   sorcery   charm
7. **incendiary**   inflammatory   flammable   combustible   catalyst   fireproof

D. Missing words

Choose the best word to complete the sentences.

The Harry Potter stories are a famous series of (1) _____ (cartoons, novels, essays) written by J.K. Rowling. They describe the life of a young wizard, who together with his friends, fought against the main (2) _____ (antagonist, protagonist, arsonist) of the story, Voldemort. The first novel was (3) _____ (claimed, achieved, published) in June 1997 and quickly became a success worldwide. The novels have been (4) _____ (written, translated, filmed) into more than seventy languages. The series comprises seven books which were eventually (5) _____ (adopted, submitted, adapted) into an eight-part movie series.

E. Odd One Out

Four of the words in each list are linked. Mark the word that is not related to these four.

Example: red   green   ~~stripy~~   blue   yellow

1.	faucet	soap	water	spoon	shampoo
2.	skirt	shirt	scissors	pants	sweater
3.	movie	ticket	popcorn	classroom	seats
4.	medicine	ointment	printer	injection	blood
5.	joy	sorrow	sunny	happy	sad

F. Idioms

Match each idiom to its meaning.

1.	**Go down in flames**	a. To be in good health
2.	**Get wind of something**	b. Brave and courageous actions are often rewarded
3.	**Fortune favours the bold**	c. To regain energy after getting tired
4.	**Fit as a fiddle**	d. To fail spectacularly
5.	**Get a second wind**	e. To become aware of a secret

Set 39

A. Synonyms

Select the word that most closely matches the meaning of the word provided.

1.	**inquisitive**	disinterested	apathetic	careless	prying	uninterested
2.	**iridescent**	monochrome	colourful	dull	plain	colourless
3.	**malevolent**	charitable	amiable	caring	sympathetic	malicious
4.	**mutiny**	rebellion	compliance	obedience	submission	subordination
5.	**timorous**	courageous	daring	diffident	bold	fearless
6.	**oblivious**	conscious	attentive	rapt	insensible	cautious
7.	**plummet**	escalate	descend	rocket	ascend	soar
8.	**prance**	trudge	cower	strut	cringe	run

B. Fill in the blanks

Fill in the blanks from the words in the table below. There are two extra words you do not need.

land	marine	insulation	posture	meticulous	entangle	blanket

1. Sea otters are endangered _____ mammals found along the coasts of Pacific

2. Ocean. They _____ themselves in seaweed to prevent themselves from being carried

   by ocean currents to the deep ocean. Sea otters have thick fur which traps air in order to

3. form a layer of _____ against cold waters. They love to sleep while floating,

4. lying on their backs in a serene _____. Sea otters love to eat marine animals.

5. However, these animals are very _____ about hygiene and clean their coats

   with their teeth and paws after eating.

C. Antonyms

Pick the word that means the opposite or near opposite of the word provided.

1.	**propitiate**	placate	flabbergast	reconcile	appease	assuage
2.	**imperious**	arrogant	servile	dictatorial	autocratic	haughty
3.	**reprieve**	punish	respite	indemnify	pardon	remit
4.	**repudiate**	renounce	retract	accept	spurn	forsake
5.	**resent**	begrudge	grudge	abominate	abhor	adore
6.	**saunter**	ramble	hasten	promenade	meander	stroll
7.	**surplus**	shortage	leftover	surfeit	spare	plethora
8.	**laconic**	pithy	compact	garrulous	concise	terse

D. Missing letters

Fill in the missing letters to complete the words in the boxes below.

1. Mayon is an | a | | t | | v | | volcano in the Philippines. It is considered the

2. world's most | | e | | r | | e | | t | volcanic cone because of its symmetrical

3. shape. Popular with | c | l | | m | | b | | r | | and campers, the volcano

4. forms the centre of a national park. Large abaca plantations grow on its | | o | | w | | r |

5. slope. There have been more than 30 eruptions | | e | | c | | | d | e | d |

since records began in 1616.

E. Homophones and homographs

Homophones are two or more words having the same pronunciation but different spellings and meanings. Homographs are words which have the same spelling but different meanings.

From the list below, fill in the blanks. (The first one has been done for you).

| censor | sensor | brace | fire | recall |

1. To get ready — brace
2. A chemical change manifested by light, flame, and heat — fire
3. To remember something that has been learned or experienced — recall
4. To dismiss from employment — fire
5. To examine something in order to remove anything considered to be objectionable — censor
6. To ask to return a defective product; to revoke — recall
7. A piece of structural material or supporting beam that serves to strengthen something — brace
8. A device that responds to a signal or stimulus and responds to it — sensor

Set 40

A. Synonyms

Select the word that most closely matches the meaning of the word provided.

1.	**shrivel**	thrive	wizen	spout	grow	evolve
2.	**convoluted**	basic	easy	clear	pleasing	intricate
3.	**tenacity**	fragility	mobility	fortitude	weakness	hesitation
4.	**underpin**	corroborate	weaken	undermine	accuse	attenuate
5.	**tethered**	adrift	free	shackled	unfastened	unbound
6.	**treachery**	devotion	allegiance	fidelity	perfidy	loyalty
7.	**trudge**	sprint	plod	glide	jog	hover

B. Fill in the blanks

Fill in the blanks from the words in the table below. There are two extra words you do not need.

important	metals	steadfast	popular	unrivalled	gemstones	hardest

1. Diamonds are _____ composed of pure carbon. They are the

2. _____ naturally occurring substance known. Because of this, diamonds have a

3. number of _____ industrial applications. Besides their industrial uses, the

4. brilliance, and sparkle of diamonds makes them _____ as jewels. In the

5. symbolism of gemstones, the diamond represents _____ love and is considered

   as the birthstone for the month of April.

C. Antonyms

Pick the word that means the opposite or near opposite of the word provided.

1. **ubiquitous**   sporadic   prevalent   omnipresent   pervasive   frequent
2. **omnipotent**   almighty   divine   powerful   vulnerable   invincible
3. **sullen**   morose   buoyant   sulky   dismal   grim
4. **equidistant**   median   average   intermediate   mode   unequal
5. **vigilant**   observant   attentive   negligent   wary   cautious
6. **contorted**   twisted   warped   straightened   askew   writhed
7. **aptitude**   capacity   inability   skill   proficiency   propensity

D. Missing words

Choose the best word to complete the sentences.

Sir Walter Raleigh, was an English (1) _____ (politician, adventurer, actor) and writer. In 1569 he (2) _____ (escaped, refused, fought) on the Huguenot side in the Wars of Religion in France. Later, his (3) _____ (outspoken, reserved, timid) criticism of the way English policy was being implemented in Ireland brought him to the attention of Queen Elizabeth He became one of her favourites and was knighted in 1585. He is best known for pioneering efforts to establish English colonies in North America. They failed and he was accused of (4) _____ (loyalty, faithful, treason) by Elizabeth's successor, James I. He was (5) _____ (imprisoned, freed, released) in the Tower of London and eventually put to death.

E. Odd One Out

Four of the words in each list are linked. Mark the word that is not related to these four.

Example: red   green   ~~stripy~~   blue   yellow

1.	dinner	lunch	snack	breakfast	supper
2.	crocodile	seal	turtle	otter	falcon
3.	sun	lava	ice	fire	heat
4.	chair	table	pencil	school	eraser
5.	ox	grasshopper	bull	hare	deer

F. Idioms

Match each idiom to its meaning.

1. **A bed of roses**   a. To focus on something irrelevant

2. **Every dog has his day**   b. An easy and comfortable situation

3. **Familiarity breeds contempt**   c. Being too curious may get you into trouble

4. **Curiosity killed the cat** d. Everyone gets a chance at some point in their lives

5. **Beat a dead horse**   e. The more you know someone, the more you become easily bored with them leading to a disrespectful relationship

Set 41

A. Synonyms

Select the word that most closely matches the meaning of the word provided.

1.	**adept**	clumsy	inept	amateur	incompetent	proficient
2.	**profuse**	scarce	frugal	exuberant	niggardly	meagre
3.	**dissuade**	incite	encourage	expostulate	abet	entice
4.	**ration**	apportion	sell	collect	monopolize	gather
5.	**credulous**	suspicious	sceptical	shrewd	susceptible	wary
6.	**fiend**	chum	villain	angel	saint	accomplice
7.	**forthright**	hypocritical	devious	secret	candid	evasive
8.	**vigour**	boredom	vitality	apathy	atrophy	coyness

B. Fill in the blanks

Fill in the blanks from the words in the table below. There are two extra words you do not need.

| pest | protect | commercial | expensive | digested | popular | ground |

1. Kopi Luwak is the most _____ coffee in the world. It is made from coffee

2. beans that are partially _____ and then pooped out by an Asian Palm Civet, a

   catlike creature. A cup of Kopi Luwak can sell for as much as $80 in the United States. In

3. Indonesia, the Asian Palm Civet, which raids _____ fruit farms, is often seen as a

4. _____ , but the growth of the Kopi Luwak industry has encouraged local people to

5. _____ Civets for their valuable dung.

C. Antonyms

Pick the word that means the opposite or near opposite of the word provided.

1.	**celestial**	astral	ethereal	seraphic	terrestrial	hallowed
2.	**sedate**	sober	frivolous	solemn	serene	tranquil
3.	**monotonous**	uninteresting	prosaic	tedious	dreary	enthralling
4.	**craven**	pusillanimous	gladiatorial	coward	chicken	dastardly
5.	**premeditate**	improvise	predetermine	intend	calculate	pause
6.	**inept**	awkward	maladroit	dexterous	unskilled	clueless
7.	**debacle**	fiasco	trouncing	triumph	drubbing	disaster
8.	**misdemeanour**	offence	infringement	misdeed	fault	obedience

D. Missing letters

Fill in the missing letters to complete the words in the boxes below.

1. Did you know that there is a wasp which turns its [ ][ ][e][y][ ] into zombies?

2. This species is named after a [ ][h][ ][r][a][ ][ ][e][r][ ] in the Harry

3. Potter movie. The Dementor wasp attacks cockroaches and [i][ ][j][e][ ][t][ ]

4. a venom into them. This blocks their neurons leaving them [ ][n][a][ ][l][ ]

5. to direct their movements but leaving them alive. Once their prey is stunned, the wasps [l][ ][r][ ] them into their shelter in order to devour them.

E. Homophones and homographs

Homophones are two or more words having the same pronunciation but different spellings and meanings. Homographs are words which have the same spelling but different meanings.

From the list below, fill in the blanks. (The first one has been done for you).

| pain | pane | row | fly | attribute |

1. To move in or pass through the air with wings — _____ fly _____
2. A series of objects arranged in a straight line — _____
3. A framed sheet of glass in a window or door — _____
4. A quality, character, or characteristic belonging to someone or something — _____
5. An unpleasant feeling or distress following an injury or disorder — _____
6. To propel a boat by means of oars — _____
7. A winged insect — _____
8. An object recognised as a symbol of a saint or mythical figure — _____

Set 42

A. Synonyms

Select the word that most closely matches the meaning of the word provided.

1. **conversant**	ignorant	cognizant	quiet	silly	inexperienced
2. **snag**	convenience	welfare	impediment	aid	assistance
3. **ruefully**	boastfully	regally	stonily	contritely	painlessly
4. **dissent**	acquiesce	concur	sanction	approve	discord
5. **furtive**	clandestine	honest	open	blatant	truthful
6. **plethora**	scarcity	dearth	paucity	surplus	deficiency
7. **appraise**	presume	measure	depreciate	devalue	deride

B. Fill in the blanks

Fill in the blanks from the words in the table below. There are two extra words you do not need.

corals	preservation	ecosystem	visible	larger	smaller	cleanliness

1. The Great Barrier Reef, the world's largest _____, is home to thousands of

2. different species of coral and marine animals. It is _____ than the Great Wall of

3. China and clearly _____ from glass bottomed tourist boats. However, the

4. Great Barrier Reef has lost more than half of its _____ due to climate change,

   pollution and fishing. As one of the Seven Wonders of the World, experts have been doing a lot

5. of planning for the reef's protection and _____.

C. Antonyms

Pick the word that has the opposite meaning of the word that has been provided.

1.	**exhort**	advise	encourage	prompt	constrain	counsel
2.	**diffident**	desirous	timorous	retiring	humble	bashful
3.	**deploy**	marshal	arrange	order	set out	withhold
4.	**extricate**	liberate	embroil	remove	extract	release
5.	**thwart**	defeat	prevent	abet	hinder	foil
6.	**fastidious**	sloppy	particular	scrupulous	finicky	careful
7.	**gravitas**	sobriety	distinction	grandeur	mischief	dignity

D. Missing words

Choose the best word to complete the sentences.

Great White Sharks are the largest (1) _____ (prey, predators, herbivores) in the world, growing up to 15 feet in length. They have a hydrodynamic (2) _____ (torpedo, tornado, tsunami) shaped body that allows them to swim at up to 15 miles per hour. They mainly (3) _____ (prey, predator, hide) on animals such as sea lions, seals, small toothed whales and turtles. A baby shark is called a (4) _____ (sharkette, pup, joey), and right after being born, they swim away from their mothers in order to hunt for small marine mammals on their own. These Great White Sharks can (5) _____ (swim, die, live) up to 70 years.

E. Odd One Out

Four of the words in each list are linked. Mark the word that is not related to these four.

Example: red   green   ~~stripy~~   blue   yellow

1.	cheese	carrots	chalk	beef	bread
2.	sweet	salty	bitter	sour	fresh
3.	tango	horror	cha-cha	samba	salsa
4.	Alabama	Alaska	Maine	Glasgow	Indiana
5.	Obama	Bush	Gandhi	Clinton	Lincoln

F. Idioms

Match each idiom to its meaning.

1.	**The calm before the storm**	a.	To make it impossible to apologise or reverse a negotiating position
2.	**To burn bridges**	b.	Something unexpected, a surprise
3.	**A bolt from the blue**	c.	Finding a solution or preventing a problem is better than trying to deal with it later
4.	**As right as rain**	d.	A very quiet, calm period before an attack, or a problem
5.	**An ounce of prevention is worth a pound of cure**	e.	In excellent condition, to be perfectly fit

Set 1: Answers & Explanations

A. Synonyms

1. turmoil — state of confusion, disturbance or disorder
2. irresponsible — not behaving in a responsible way
3. imperturbability -- calmness, cannot be upset
4. adept — very skilled at something; expert
5. flagrant — an extremely offensive action
6. vernacular — the special language spoken by natives of a certain place or region
7. wander — to move about without a specific goal or purpose
8. cliff — a vertical rock face

B. Fill in the blanks

1. strike
2. torrential – rain falling rapidly and violently
3. evacuate – help people to leave an area
4. injured
5. smashed

C. Antonyms

1. pleasant
2. cowardly
3. simple
4. solemn
5. acceptable
6. salubrious
7. cheerful
8. extraordinary

D. Missing letters

1. useful
2. nutritious
3. liquid
4. beverage
5. various

E. Homophones and homographs

1. address
2. maze
3. master
4. address
5. master
6. race
7. race
8. maize

Set 2: Answers & Explanations

A. Synonyms

1. languid — a person with slow movement; weak; frail
2. bottom — the lowest point of a situation
3. ferocious — extreme fierceness; violent
4. obscure — cannot be clearly understood; uncertain
5. petulant — behaving rudely; bad tempered
6. bring about — cause something to happen
7. denounce — to publicly express displeasure at someone

B. Fill in the blanks

1. interesting   2. queue   3. nauseous   4. herbivorous   5. extinct

C. Antonyms

1. forbidden   2. pleased   3. keep out   4. whisper
5. common   6. abase   7. reluctance

D. Choose the correct missing word

1. crops   2. took   3. respectively   4. manor   5. wore

E. Odd one out

1. flute — a flute is a wind instrument, the rest are stringed instruments
2. airplane — all the means of transport are used on water except airplane
3. cry — all the emotions are expressions of happiness, except cry
4. tongue — all the words are parts of the eye except tongue
5. equation — is an expression used in algebra while the others are all actions performed in arithmetic

F. Idioms

1. b   2. a   3. e   4. d   5. c

Set 3: Answers & Explanations

A. Synonyms

1. rebuke — to criticise someone; express disapproval of someone
2. recondite — cannot be easily understood; uncertain
3. nervous — not calm
4. cooperation — working together with someone
5. emotional — poignant means sad which is being emotional
6. greed — wanting more than enough for yourself
7. relieved — reduced severity of something e.g. symptoms of an illness
8. eradicate — to pull something up by its roots; to eliminate

B. Fill in the blanks

1. clinched
2. sweep — to win a series of games
3. dominant
4. crucial
5. twice

C. Antonyms

1. affection
2. bulging
3. descent
4. dissent
5. revere
6. stammer
7. whole
8. fleshy

D. Missing letters

1. stocky
2. largest
3. streams
4. garbage
5. torpor

E. Homophones and homographs

1. moose
2. waste
3. stake
4. fall
5. steak
6. mousse
7. fall
8. waist

Set 4: Answers & Explanations

A. Synonyms

1. provoke — to stir up something on purpose; stimulate
2. unbelief — finding something amazing, impossible to believe
3. obsession — focusing on something to the exclusion of everything else
4. voracious — having a huge appetite; excessively eager
5. audacious — bold; daring; fearless
6. confirmed — something that is done by habit; a confirmed pattern of behaviour
7. flexible — something which can change shape or posture easily

B. Fill in the blanks

1. latest 2. reigning 3. match 4. reached 5. upsets

C. Antonyms

1. generous 2. frugal 3. immigrant 4. powerless
5. grieve 6. stoic 7. reprimand

D. Missing words

1. different 2. tropical 3. native 4. distributed 5. cultivated

E. Odd one out

1. umbrella -- All are clothes are used during bad weather except umbrella.
2. snow - -- All the words are about summer except snow which falls in winter.
3. mountain — All the features are manmade structures except for mountain.
4. dolphin -- All the creatures are reptiles or amphibians except dolphin.
5. car -- All are items are pieces of furniture while a car is a means of transport.

F. Idioms

1. d 2. c 3. b 4. e 5. a

Set 5: Answers & Explanations

A. Synonyms

1. vivid — a sharp, intense image; clear
2. innumerable — too many to count
3. subtle — a state that cannot be easily perceived
4. servile — slavery; excessive desire to do something for others
5. sickly — unhealthy usually with a pale, pallid skin
6. scrutinise — examine; search or inspect something
7. plague — a widespread disease; something that causes disturbance and irritation
8. stupendous — awesome; marvellous; amazing

B. Fill in the blanks

1. species   2. useful   3. colonies   4. kinds   5. wings

C. Antonyms

1. surrender — cease to resist instead of fighting back by pummelling somebody
2. mainstream — an idea, attitude or activity that is done normally or conventionally
3. straightforward -- not difficult or hard work
4. negligent — failing to take care of something properly
5. assertive — confident, bold, firm personality
6. conformist — following a set of beliefs which heretics deny
7. orthodoxy — a generally accepted theory, doctrine or practice
8. loosely — not exactly like all the other words

D. Missing letters

1. related   2. energy   3. range   4. plants   5. smallest

E. Homophones and homographs

1. bark   2. wave   3. spell   4. wave
5. spell   6. sail   7. bark   8. sale

Set 6: Answers & Explanations

A. Synonyms

1. strip — to rob; loot
2. puncture -- a small hole
3. sabotage — to damage an enemy's property to prevent their success
4. insane — insane/mad people often carried out frenzied attacks
5. cloudy — difficult to see through (of a liquid)
6. furious — angry or unstable
7. courageous -- brave

B. Fill in the blanks

1. composed	2. oxygen	3. absorbs	4. divided

5. troposphere — lowest region of the atmosphere and nearest to the earth's surface

C. Antonyms

1. lovely	2. depressed	3. foreign	4. low
5. novice	6. certainty	7. dissonance	

D. Missing words

1. was	2. unanimously	3. known	4. implemented	5. led

E. Odd one out

1. chess — All the words are ball games except for chess which is a board game.
2. ballad -- All the words are movie genres except ballad which is a music genre.
3. gloves — All the words are footwear except gloves which are for the hands.
4. paper — All the words are used for writing while paper is used to write on.
5. telephone — All the words are parts of the house except telephone.

F: Idioms

1. c	2. e	3. a	4. b	5. d

Set 7: Answers & Explanations

A. Synonyms

1. cling — to hold on tightly to
2. achievable — possible, practical
3. light — a beacon is a powerful light
4. bliss — extreme happiness
5. pinnacle — the highest point
6. murky — a liquid that is cloudy, dirty, opaque or muddy
7. delightful — very nice
8. concise — brief words but full of information

B. Fill in the blanks

1. liner — a large ship designed to carry passengers
2. unsinkable
3. deemed
4. voyage — the journey of a ship
5. hit

C. Antonyms

1. insignificant   2. construct   3. fictitious   4. insanity   5. candidate
6. attractive   7. continuation   8. incarcerate

D. Missing letters

1. honour   2. defeated   3. commemoration — a remembrance ceremony for a person or an event
4. parades   5. federal — something related to the national government and applying to the whole country

E. Homophones and homographs

1. hare   2. patient   3. hair   4. patient   5. kind
6. kind   7. mine   8. mine

Set 8: Answers & Explanations

A. Synonyms

1. pungent — a strong, sharp taste or smell
2. haul — to drag or pull
3. pacify — to bring peace to; to calm someone
4. lament — to express grief or sorrow
5. benevolent — kind, warm-hearted person or a charitable organization
6. vagabond — do not have a permanent residence and moves from place to place
7. humongous — something big or huge

B. Fill in the blanks

1. before   2. tradition   3. include   4. originated   5. ward

C. Antonyms

1. gullible   2. wild   3. artifice   4. upright   5. prolong
6. careless   7. delighted

D. Missing words

1. expelled – being thrown out or kicked out of school   2. loved
3. awarded   4. equation   5. taught – past tense of teach

E. Odd one out

1. valley — All the words are bodies of water except valley which is dry land.
2. bicycle — All the words are four-wheeled vehicles except bicycle.
3. cabbage — All the words are fruits except cabbage which is a vegetable.
4. dog — All the animals belong to the feline family except for dog.
5. cake — All the words are drinks except cake which is food.

F: Idioms

1. d   2. a   3. e   4. c   5. b

Set 9: Answers & Explanations

A. Synonyms

1. optimistic	– someone who is hopeful and confident of the future
2. capitulate	– to surrender to an opponent
3. capricious	– a sudden change in behaviour or mood
4. appetising	– something which makes you want to eat it
5. stormy	– bad weather with strong winds, heavy rain and sometimes thunder
6. vociferous	– a person who seeks attention by being loud and insistent
7. examine	– to look at or check something carefully
8. degenerate	– a decline in one's physical, mental or moral qualities

B. Fill in the blanks

1. highest   2. border   3. glaciers – rivers of ice   4. inhabited   5. summit

C. Antonyms

1. decent	– good behaviour
2. ascetic	– someone who lives simply, often to follow a religion
3. apprentice	– someone who is learning from a skilled craftsman
4. punctual	– to be on time
5. literary	– formal, scholarly
6. brutish	– bad, or violent behaviour
7. obnoxious	– smelly or unpleasant
8. answer	– the solution to a conundrum

D. Missing letters

1. eliminate   2. reuse   3. reduce   4. recycle   5. maintain

E. Homophones and homographs

1. loan   2. lap   3. like   4. bat
5. like   6. lap   7. lone   8. bat

Set 10: Answers & Explanations

A. Synonyms

1. catastrophe — a disaster; fiasco; something that causes great damage
2. arrest — when the police apprehend/catch a criminal
3. frontier — a line or border separating countries
4. disturbing -- upsetting
5. echo — a reflection of sound; an imitation of someone's idea, movement, style
6. force — use physical means or mental pressure to make somebody do some
7. difference — a discrepancy is the difference between what is expected and reality

B. Fill in the blanks

| 1. incorporated | 2. fossils | 3. geologists | 4. crust | 5. drift |

C. Antonyms

| 1. stagnant | 2. escape | 3. crude | 4. public | 5. niggardly |
| 6. tax | 7. cowardly |

D. Choose the correct missing word

| 1. known | 2. ability | 3. control | 4. disguise | 5. unpredictable |

E. Odd one out

1. plane — All the words are natural phenomena seen in the sky except a plane
2. bat — All the words are birds except bat which is a mammal.
3. car — All the words are vehicles used in water while cars are found on land.
4. ivory — All the words are metals except ivory which comes from elephants.
5. nod — All are movements are made with the legs except to nod.

F: Idioms

| 1. c | 2. a | 3. d | 4. e | 5. b |

Set 11: Answers & Explanations

A. Synonyms

1. naïve — someone who lacks experience
2. cunning — someone who is devious or scheming
3. agitation — a state of anxiety
4. versatile — flexible; able to adapt to different situations
5. intrude — to disrupt
6. affront — to insult someone
7. quip — a witty remark
8. danger -- the absence of safety

B. Fill in the blanks

| 1. similar | 2. equipment | 3. catch | 4. class | 5. popular |

C. Antonyms

| 1. unrelated | 2. proof | 3. confusing | 4. averse |
| 5. preserved | 6. open | 7. plethora | 8. modern |

D. Missing letters

| 1. mysteries | 2. disappeared | 3. attribute | 4. proof |
| 5. navigate |

E. Homophones and homographs

| 1. incite | 2. pound | 3. firm | 4. count |
| 5. firm | 6. pound | 7. insight | 8. count |

Set 12: Answers & Explanations

A. Synonyms

1. hindrance – something that causes delay
2. comical – a funny act; amusing
3. delectable – delicious; delightful; highly pleasing
4. absurd – silly or ridiculous
5. extinguish – put out (a fire)
6. bizarre – unusual or odd
7. uncontrolled – not under control

B. Fill in the blanks

1. ruled 2. celebrated 3. monarch 4. accord 5. head

C. Antonyms

1. ailing – someone who is sick or injured
2. sensible – not stupid, considered
3. distant – unfriendly
4. contemptuous – showing disrespect
5. straighten – to remove twists; untwine
6. intermittently – occurring irregularly
7. natty – someone who is neat and appears smart

D. Missing letters

1. defined 2. cause 3. trapped 4. prevent 5. planting

E. Odd one out

1. farm – All the words are types of houses except farm.
2. refrigerator – A refrigerator is a machine while others are not.
3. chest – All the words are parts of the face except for the chest.
4. stone – All the words are living things except stone.
5. umbrella – All the items are powered by electricity except for umbrella which is manually operated.

F: Idioms

1. d 2. a 3. e 4. b 5. c

Set 13: Answers & Explanations

A. Synonyms

1. scanty — small or insufficient in amount
2. queer — something strange or odd
3. disorder — physical or mental sickness/malady
4. harassed — to be annoyed by someone on a regular basis
5. elaborate — make more complicated
6. opponent -- enemy
7. vulgar — unrefined, loud, rude
8. hindrance — something which stops or discourages somebody from doing something

B. Fill in the blanks

| 1. originated | 2. tropical | 3. experts | 4. rich | 5. improving |

C. Antonyms

| 1. authentic | 2. resist | 3. dauntless | 4. fact |
| 5. negligent | 6. frivolous | 7. slack | 8. arrogant |

D. Missing letters

| 1. known | 2. sense | 3. sensitive | 4. emotions | 5. companions |

E. Homophones and homographs

| 1. rain | 2. project | 3. bill | 4. project |
| 5. reign | 6. scale | 7. bill | 8. scale |

Set 14: Answers & Explanations

A. Synonyms

1. wheedle – to flatter someone
2. shroud – something that covers
3. deliberate – to think carefully
4. control – to limit/curb
5. indigent – poor, needy, penniless
6. debase – reduce, degrade
7. evade – avoid, ignore, reject

B. Fill in the blanks

1. atoll – a ring shaped island made of corals
2. ocean
3. natives
4. tourists
5. vegetation

C. Antonyms

1. feast
2. potent
3. real
4. demure
5. severe
6. clumsy
7. compliant

D. Missing words

1. strength
2. demigod – a child of a god and mortal; someone who has some but not all powers of a god
3. raised
4. difficulty
5. warrior

E. Odd one out

1. fish – All the species are amphibians except fish which live only in water.
2. circle – All the shapes are formed with straight lines except circles.
3. ally – All the words are synonyms while ally is their antonym
4. radio – All the words are musical instruments except radio which is a listening device.
5. ounces – All the words are currencies except ounces which are a unit of weight.

F: Idioms

1. c
2. e
3. d
4. b
5. a

Set 15: Answers & Explanations

A. Synonyms

1. contradictory — at opposite ends of a spectrum
2. dull — not shiny
3. douse — cover something completely in water
4. venture — to show initiative/enterprise
5. restrained — moderate, controlled
6. pierce — to make a hole with a sharp object
7. suppress — stop, put an end to
8. hypocrisy — pretending to believe one thing and doing another

B. Fill in the blanks

1. built   2. ruler   3. tombs   4. man-made   5. unsurpassed

C. Antonyms

1. turn in (a criminal) -- refuse to provide them with a place of safety/harbour
2. significant — enough to make a difference therefore not trivial
3. democrat — someone who rules according to the will of the people
4. candour — being frank, open and honest
5. surrender — to give up, stop whatever you are endeavouring to do
6. pleasure — a pleasant experience
7. befuddle — to confuse someone
8. kill — to cause the death or failure of

D. Missing letters

1. rainforest   2. comprises   3. ecosystem   4. important   5. absorb

E. Homophones and homographs

1. soul   2. ring   3. sole   4. minute
5. crane   6. minute   7. ring   8. crane

Set 16: Answers & Explanations

A. Synonyms

1. arid – dry, little to no rain
2. hazard – a source of danger
3. hasty – quick; fast
4. inaugurate – to introduce, implement
5. rootless – to have no place to call home
6. unravel – to solve; to clarify something
7. impudent – disrespectful

B. Fill in the blanks

1. combination
2. dorsal – upper side or back
3. anchor – to hold on to
4. protect
5. hermaphrodites – a creature which is both male and female

C. Antonyms

1. simple
2. unite
3. satisfied
4. jittery
5. be blunt
6. belligerent
7. valley

D. Missing words

1. massive
2. seen
3. belongs
4. tremendous
5. felled

E. Odd one out

1. biology – All the subjects are branches of mathematics except biology.
2. rabbit – All the creatures lay eggs except for rabbits.
3. stove – All the items are used for dining except a stove is used for cooking.
4. wolf – All the animals can be pets except wolves which are wild animals.
5. sugar – All the foodstuffs are spices except sugar.

F: Idioms

1. d
2. e
3. b
4. a
5. c

Set 17: Answers & Explanations

A. Synonyms

1. debilitated — someone who is weak and lacks energy
2. trivial — worthless; empty; unimportant
3. imbibe — to drink (usually alcohol)
4. hillock — a small hill
5. remedy — a solution or treatment
6. gratify — satisfy a desire
7. tremble — shake with fear or cold
8. picturesque — very attractive; striking appearance

B. Fill in the blanks

1. known   2. parasitic   3. extinction   4. possess   5. corolla

C. Antonyms

1. adamant — someone who has made a decision that cannot be changed
2. defiant — refusing to yield
3. negligent — careless, not paying attention
4. repudiate — refuse to accept
5. confidant — sure you know the right answer
6. gracious — good mannered, polite
7. abstemious — refraining from an activity
8. righteousness — the condition of doing what is right

D. Missing letters

1. bird   2. stride   3. feathers   4. herd   5. dominant

E. Homophones and homographs

1. object   2. palm   3. canvass   4. palm
5. contract   6. contract   7. canvas   8. object

Set 18: Answers & Explanations

A. Synonyms

1. comply — to follow the correct rules or procedures
2. scrape — to rub something in a way which makes its surface uneven
3. diminution — to reduce in size
4. forgiveness — to accept an apology
5. coerce — to force someone
6. conciseness — being brief and to the point
7. naive — innocent, inexperienced

B. Fill in the blanks

1. native to ……. – the country of origin of a species
2. larger
3. flap – move up and down (of a bird's wings)
4. habitat – an animal's home environment
5. plumage – collective term for bird's feathers

C. Antonyms

1. solitude	2. repel	3. absence	4. hero
5. rush	6. clever	7. neglect	

D. Missing words

1. unknown   2. sternum – breastbone   3. symbol   4. logo   5. commonly

E. Odd one out

1. guava — Only guava is a fruit. All the others are vegetables.
2. pink — All the colours are found in the rainbow except pink.
3. goat — All the words are baby animals except goat which is an adult.
4. knife — All the words are containers used to collect water except knife.
5. dam — All the words are natural phenomena except dam which is manmade.

F: Idioms

1. c   2. d   3. a   4. e   5. b

Set 19: Answers & Explanations

A. Synonyms

1. diminish — to decrease or lessen
2. grind — tedious work/drudgery
3. fool — a stupid person
4. dismal — depressing
5. rejoice — be happy
6. provoke — to stimulate
7. laugh — to show amusement
8. avaricious -- greedy

B. Fill in the blanks

1. situated   2. ratified   3. construction   4. withstand   5. earthquakes

C. Antonyms

1. humble — not pretentious
2. entitlement — having the right to do something
3. loyalty — (in politics) showing support for the existing regime
4. parched — to make something extremely dry by exposing it to extreme heat
5. depressed -- sad
6. brazen — shameless; bold
7. conspicuous — be visible, to gain attention
8. lengthy -- (of a text) too long

D. Missing letters

1. reptile   2. outside   3. source   4. attract   5. stealth

E. Homophones and homographs

1. cabinet   2. week   3. chest   4. pen
5. weak   6. pen   7. cabinet   8. chest

Set 20: Answers & Explanations

A. Synonyms

1. arsenal — store/depot for weapons used by an army
2. remunerative — financially rewarding
3. askew — not straight or level
4. outcast — a person rejected by society
5. frightful -- scary
6. shabby — in very old, worn or poor condition
7. clutter — mess, litter

B. Fill in the blanks

| 1. amphibian | 2. beneath | 3. tropical | 4. underside | 5. insects |

C. Antonyms

| 1. moribund | 2. apologist | 3. fact | 4. amenable |
| 5. groomed | 6. being | 7. interesting | |

D. Missing words

| 1. extremely | 2. hence | 3. contrary | 4. originated | 5. infer |

E. Odd one out

1. lotus — Only the lotus plant grows in water.
2. bed — All the items are used inside the classroom except for bed.
3. June — All the months have 31 days except June with 30 days.
4. nephew — All the people are example of couples except for nephew.
5. friend — All the people are part of a family except for friend.

F: Idioms

| 1. e | 2. a | 3. b | 4. c | 5. d |

Set 21: Answers & Explanations

A. Synonyms

1. dreary — dull, uninteresting
2. compliant — willing to follow a set of rules
3. headland — a narrow piece of land jutting out into the sea
4. clement — someone with merciful actions
5. pretend — be something other than who you really are
6. flashy — impressive; vulgar; attracting attention with extravagant and expensive things
7. flowers — the everyday word for flora
8. giddy — dizzy, silly

B. Fill in the blanks

1. measures   2. reservoir   3. power   4. industry   5. stunning

C. Antonyms

1. active   2. anxious   3. forbid   4. sophisticated
5. enlighten   6. acquaint   7. juvenile   8. firm

D. Missing letters

1. bipedal – someone who uses two legs for walking   2. fearsome – frightening
3. weighed   4. named   5. found

E. Homophones and homographs

1. gate   2. desert   3. dessert   4. box
5. spare   6. gait   7. box   8. spare

Set 22: Answers & Explanations

A. Synonyms

1. parade   2. indefinite   3. uniform   4. combative
5. transformation 6. first   7. surrogate

B. Fill in the blanks

1. wholly   2. elusive – difficult to find or achieve   3. curl – roll tightly
4. nocturnal – active at night   5. trafficked - involved in illegal trade

C. Antonyms

1. submissive   not willing to resist
2. obvious   not difficult to understand
3. slight   not steep or sudden
4. forgetful   absent minded
5. fundamental   essential, not trivial
6. balanced   even handed, measured, not frenetic
7. excellent   very good

D. Missing words

1. species   2. float   3. rows   4. concentrate   5. contact

E. Odd one out

1. eggplant   – All the vegetables are root crops except for eggplant.
2. page   – All the words are parts of language except page.
3. salad   – All the foods are cooked by baking except salad.
4. lizard   – All the species can fly except for lizards which crawl.
5. Finland   – All the countries are in Asia except Finland which is in Europe.

F: Idioms

1. b   2. d   3. a   4. e   5. c

Set 23: Answers & Explanations

A. Synonyms

1. escape — get out of somewhere without permission e.g. a prison
2. judicious — having good sense of judgment
3. prudent — wise, someone who cares of future
4. substandard — (in grading academic work) poor, unsatisfactory
5. caprice — sudden change of behaviour
6. enmity — a feeling of hatred or ill-will
7. amorous — romantic, passionate
8. pernicious — causing great harm; deadly

B. Fill in the blanks

| 1. bookshelves | 2. purchased | 3. volumes | 4. houses | 5. turn |

C. Antonyms

| 1. commendable | 2. indoor | 3. give | 4. inert |
| 5. virtuous | 6. predecessor | 7. distant | 8. repulsive |

D. Misisng letters

1. slither — to slide or glide
2. discovered — found for the first time
3. vertebral - with a backbone
4. debate — academic discussion
5. evolved — changed slowly over a long period of time

E. Homophones and homographs

| 1. mind | 2. peel | 3. buckle | 4. mind |
| 5. hatch | 6. peal | 7. buckle | 8. hatch |

Set 24: Answers & Explanations

A. Synonyms

1. non-believing — Atheists are non-believers in the existance of God
2. divine — describing the attributes of a God or Gods
3. hostile -- unfriendly
4. barren — fruitless, infertile, unproductive
5. dismal — depressing, gloomy, dull
6. colossal — something very large, massive
7. applause — a way of showing appreciation or giving an accolade

B. Fill In The Blanks

1. weird
2. inhabitant
3. incisors — front teeth used for cutting
4. consists
5. hind (quarters) — part of the body at the back of an animal

C. Antonyms

1. eager
2. legalize
3. remain
4. deter
5. concentrate
6. frantic
7. sympathy

D. Missing words

1. general
2. became
3. school
4. settled
5. paternal

E. Odd one out

1. sun — All the words are planets except for sun.
2. stone — All the objects are lighter than water except stone.
3. lettuces — All the foods are fruits except for lettuces.
4. oasis — All the geographical features are related to the sea except oasis.
5. Europe — All the words are languages except Europe.

F: Idioms

1. b
2. a
3. e
4. c
5. d

Set 25: Answers & Explanations

A. Synonyms

1. adversary — opponent, rival, enemy
2. shrewd — intelligent, smart, clever
3. candid — truthful, frank
4. comfort — to make something less burdensome or painful
5. fiery — burning or passionate
6. volatile — something that changes easily
7. ricochet — to rebound
8. unkempt — untidy; disorderly; sloppy

B. Fill in the blanks

1. pseudonym – a false name used by authors
2. scientist
3. draft
4. diplomat – a representative of a country
5. elegance

C. Antonyms

1. effortless
2. plump
3. feasible
4. obese
5. appealing
6. flatness
7. amenable
8. dissension

D. Missing letters

1. drowsy – half-asleep
2. resemble
3. hanging
4. sluggish – slow moving
5. domain – habitat, a place of living

E. Homophones and homographs

1. charge
2. mole
3. hangar
4. charge
5. refrain
6. mole
7. hanger
8. refrain

Set 26: Answers & Explanations

A. Synonyms

1. propriety – respectable, conventionally correct
2. charitable – willing to help others
3. amiable – being friendly, affectionate
4. devout – someone with deep religious feeling or commitment
5. shove – push or jostle somebody
6. hesitant - reluctant to make a decision, indecisive
7. gaiety – the state of being cheerful or merry

B. Fill in the blanks

1. fifth   2. mythology – the legends of an ancient culture   3. discovered
4. composed   5. massive

C. Antonyms

1. repelling   2. extinguish   3. stillness   4. flattering
5. introvert   6. pernicious   7. concrete

D. Missing words

1. uninterrupted   2. aviator   3. between   4. scarce   5. inspired

E. Odd one out

1. oxygen – All the items are solid except for oxygen which is a gas.
2. laptop – All the items are non digital personal items except laptop.
3. barber – All the occupations except barber work on a building site.
4. bridge – All the devices except bridge are used for up and down movement.
5. iron – All the others are non-metals except iron.

F: Idioms

1. c   2. e   3. b   4. d   5. a

Set 27: Answers & Explanations

A. Synonyms

1. gardener — someone who works in a garden or nursery
2. hazy — misty, unclear
3. gaudy — extravagantly showy or flashy
4. meticulous — very careful and precise
5. confusing -- unclear
6. surmise — believe without solid proof
7. tranquil — undisturbed, calm
8. perilous -- dangerous

B. Fill in the blanks

1. canine – a member of the dog family
2. robust – strong and healthy
3. scavengers – animal which feed on dead material
4. build
5. extinct

C. Antonyms

1. equity
2. restricted
3. incite
4. decipher – to interpret something
5. inferiority
6. undress
7. pleasant
8. honesty

D. Missing letters

1. extinct
2. reptiles
3. aquatic – living in water
4. quadrupeds – animals that walk using four feet
5. juvenile – young

E. Homophones and homographs

1. fuse
2. coach
3. dough
4. discount
5. fuse
6. doe
7. discount
8. coach

Set 28: Answers & Explanations

A. Synonyms

1. night — a period of darkness
2. stability — the condition of equilibrium
3. conceited — vain, big headed
4. accountable — responsible for the consequences of ones actions
5. donor — someone who gives
6. acquit — to decide that somebody is not guilty of a crime
7. implicate — to accuse someone

B. Fill in the blanks

1. coastal   2. ivory   3. source   4. capability   5. underwater

C. Antonyms

1. confirm   2. timidity   3. blunt   4. ingenuous – innocent or unsuspecting
5. give   6. utopia – an imagined place of perfection   7. harmonious

D. Missing words

1. second   2. shines   3. similar   4. consists   5. evaporates

E. Odd one out

1. jeans — All the items of clothing are footwear except jeans.
2. socks — All the items of clothing are worn on the upper body except socks.
3. centimeter — All the units measure weight except centimeter.
4. explosion — All the phenomena are natural disaters except explosion.
5. mile — All are units measure time except for mile.

F: Idioms

1. a   2. c   3. d   4. e   5. b

Set 29: Answers & Explanations

A. Synonyms

1. parable — a simple story with a moral lesson
2. strident — harsh; loud; shrill
3. cultivable — land on which crops can grow
4. pale — weak colour e.g. of skin complexion
5. affliction — causing pain and suffering
6. typhoon — a strong wind or tempest
7. grimace — an expression of disgust
8. insubstantial — weak, easily breakable

B. Fill in the blanks

1. considered
2. orbit — to move around or encircle
3. surface
4. equator — a line that divides a planet into northern and southern hemispheres
5. gathered

C. Antonyms

1. essence
2. brawny
3. despondent
4. demolish
5. audacious
6. indispensable
7. lukewarm
8. sensitive

D. Missing letters

1. peculiar
2. nocturnal
3. trees
4. enormous
5. primate — group of mammals that are the most intelligent and developed

E. Homophones and homographs

1. heir
2. date
3. company
4. defect
5. company
6. date
7. defect
8. air

Set 30: Answers & Explanations

A. Synonyms

1. permeate — something that could spread through easily
2. pummel — to strike repeatedly
3. affray — fighting in a public place that disturbs the peace
4. buoyant — cheerful and optimistic
5. wistful — nostalgic, a feeling of longing and regret
6. pungent — having a strong, penetrating smell
7. hesitation — a moral doubt about something

B. Fill in the blanks

1. freshwater   2. resemble   3. aquatic   4. derived   5. exclusively

C. Antonyms

1. reality   2. preclude – to prevent from happening   3. caution
4. endorse   5. gargantuan – enormous   6. forthcoming – about to happen
7. stiff – difficult to bend

D. Missing words

1. omnivore   2. unique   3. personalities   4. knock   5. prying

E. Odd one out

1. calculator — All the items are used in writing except calculator.
2. ostrich — All the birds can fly except ostrich.
3. iodine — All the chemicals are gases except iodine which is a liquid.
4. banana — All the fruits are juicy except banana
5. angle — All the geometric expressions relate to a circle except for angle.

F: Idioms

1. c   2. d   3. a   4. e   5. b

Set 31: Answers & Explanations

A. Synonyms

1. vulgar -- unrefined
2. allot – to distribute
3. elude – escape, evade
4. perplexity – confusion, difficulty
5. parade – put on public display
6. mutilate – to inflict violence, to cripple
7. interim – for the meantime; meanwhile
8. discernment – the ability to judge well

B. Fill in the blanks

1. freedom
2. gift
3. same
4. inscribed – carved or written
5. landmark

C. Antonyms

1. delightful
2. single
3. alluring
4. pleased
5. subordinate
6. ominous
7. meek
8. ethical

D. Missing letters

1. bear – carry or show
2. colour
3. shorter
4. herbivores – animals who feed on plants
5. endangered – at risk of becoming extinct

E. Homophones and homographs

1. compact
2. foot
3. heal
4. bar
5. foot
6. heel
7. bar
8. compact

Set 32: Answers & Explanations

A. Synonyms

1. expand — enlarge, get bigger
2. sanctuary — a place of refuge
3. betrothal — engaged to be married
4. luscious — having a delicious taste
5. reasonable — something acceptable after thinking about it
6. delight — happiness
7. tolerable -- acceptable

B. Fill in the blanks

1. unique   2. confused   3. chamber   4. scientific   5. limbs

C. Antonyms

1. expedite — to speed up action
2. prudent — a wise action
3. judicious — a good judgment; wise decision
4. concur — to agree with
5. yield — give way
6. juvenile — young, teenage
7. jovial — cheerful; happy

D. Missing words

1. richest   2. magnificent   3. unique   4. built   5. century

E. Odd one out

1. gloves — All the clothes are worn in the head except gloves.
2. nursery — All are related to education except nursery which may relate to plants.
3. boy — All the words have the same gender except boy.
4. forest — All the words are bodies of water except forest.
5. oven — All the words are parts of a car except oven.

F: Idioms

1. b   2. e   3. d   4. c   5. a

Set 33: Answers & Explanations

A. Synonyms

1. clot — form a lump
2. asphyxiate — to kill someone by depriving them of air
3. oscillate — to swing/turn at a regular speed
4. lie — to lie under oath
5. predecessor — a person who previously occupied a position
6. zealot — someone who is extremely devoted; extremist
7. vindicate — to clear someone of blame or crime
8. holocaust — a mass destruction

B. Fill in the blanks

1. junction
2. massive
3. remnant
3. endorheic — a drainage or basin without any outlet or exit
5. natural gas

C. Antonyms

1. resurrection
2. exceptional
3. divide
4. composed
5. marginal
6. reasonable
7. limited
8. clumsy

D. Missing letters

1. unearthed — to find through digging
2. limestone
3. inside
4. colour
5. microorganisms — a tiny living thing, usually a bacteria, fungi or algae

E. Homophones and homographs

1. pupil
2. whack
3. rock
4. close
5. pupil
6. wax
7. close
8. rock

Set 34: Answers & Explanations

A. Synonyms

1. dehydrate — reduce the amount of liquid in something
2. crack — a small gap
3. turmoil — a condition of disturbance, commotion
4. accord — to give someone; to present; to agree with
5. fluctuate — an irregular rise and fall in number
6. occur — happen
7. era — a long, indefinite period of time

B. Fill in the blanks

1. prehistoric
2. cannibals
3. palaeontologists – scientists who study fossils
4. ancestors
5. bizarre – strange or unusual

C. Antonyms

1. magnify
2. improve
3. even tempered
4. pardon
5. endure
6. break
7. imminent

D. Missing words

1. eighth
2. blue
3. massive
4. coldest
5. retrograde – move backwards

E. Odd one out

1. grumpy — All the emotions are positive except grumpy.
2. rice — All the foods are meat except rice.
3. dinosaur — All of the animals are living except dinosaurs which are extinct.
4. chicken — All the creatures are animals except chicken which is a bird.
5. train — All the words are forms of road transport except train

F: Idioms

1. c
2. d
3. e
4. a
5. b

Set 35: Answers & Explanations

A. Synonyms

1. delusion — a false idea about reality
2. fervent — very hot; someone who shows great intensity of feeling
3. evidently — clear, obvious
4. fecund — capable of producing an offspring; intellectually productive
5. wretched — in very bad condition, very sad
6. recumbent — lying down; horizontal
7. demented — someone who behaves irrationally; mad; insane
8. treacherous — someone who betrays or is deceitful

B. Fill in the blanks

1. indigenous – native to one place
2. pouch
3. cradle
4. balance
5. stomp

C. Antonyms

1. dissuade
2. slouch
3. needless
4. spendthrift
5. relish
6. abbreviate
7. extemporize
8. conceal

D. Missing letters

1. plateau
2. rainfall
3. moisture
4. source
5. compound

E. Homophones and homographs

1. down
2. sum
3. left
4. blunt
5. some
6. down
7. blunt
8. left

Set 36: Answers & Explanations

A. Synonyms

1. assailant – someone who physically attacks another person
2. entice – to tempt someone; to lure someone by offering a reward
3. bill – an itemised statement of money due for items purchased
4. indifferent – not caring about something, apathetic towards it
5. despotic – tyrannical; state of ruling with absolute power
6. desire – want something
7. amiss – inappropriate, done in a wrong way

B. Fill in the blanks

1. massive
2. surrounding
3. legend
4. buried
5. cured

C. Antonyms

1. applaud
2. support
3. expert
4. silence
5. dishonour
6. destroy
7. disperse

D. Missing words

1. festival
2. ancient
3. honour
4. guide
5. decorate

E. Odd one out

1. Tokyo – All the words are countries except Tokyo which is a city.
2. water – All are nouns are countable except water.
3. snake – All the species are birds except snake.
4. pitch – All are related to basketball except pitch which is used for soccer, cricket or rugby but not basketball.
5. television – All the words are related to studying except television.

F: Idioms

1. b
2. e
3. a
4. c
5. d

Set 37: Answers & Explanations

A. Synonyms

1. possibility — a small likelihood
2. fraudulent — an action done with deception or involving deception
3. cleft — divided; split
4. haphazard — lacking organization; unplanned; disorderly
5. sly — someone who is cunning or tricky
6. literate — a person who is able to read and write
7. squander — to spend carelessly; to waste something in a reckless manner
8. ideology -- a set of beliefs which is viewed as unquestionable

B. Fill in the blanks

1. rarest
2. shoots
3. broad
4. born
5. hibernate — to sleep throughout winter

C. Antonyms

1. definite
2. reimburse
3. antecedent
4. source
5. interior
6. extrovert
7. sedentary — staying in one place
8. outspoken

D. Missing letters

1. feisty
2. pudgy
3. carrion
4. spin
5. hollow

E. Homophones and homographs

1. bruise
2. solution
3. minor
4. brews
5. batter
6. minor
7. solution
8. batter

Set 38: Answers & Explanations

A. Synonyms

1. crude — in a natural state; unrefined; offensive, rude
2. ebullient — cheerful and full of energy
3. clique — a small group of friends
4. vehemence — a display of strong emotions; passionate
5. tumult — to cause confusion or disorder
6. redundant — (in language teaching) extra words with no meaning, verbosity
7. indifferent — not interested

B. Fill in the blanks

1. invented   2. experimenting   3. observed   4. piloted   5. sceptical

C. Antonyms

1. clear cut   2. smooth   3. aesthetic   4. reflection
5. decent   6. science   7. fireproof

D. Missing words

1. novels
2. antagonist – an enemy or rival usually seen in movies or books
3. published -- printing of book for public distribution and sale
4. translated
5. adapted – to alter for a movie, film or stage

E. Odd one out

1. spoon — All the items are used in the bathroom except spoon.
2. scissors — All the items are clothes except scissors.
3. classroom — All the items are related to the theatre except classroom.
4. printer — All the items are related to hospitals except printer.
5. sunny — All the words are emotions except sunny.

F: Idioms

1. d   2. e   3. b   4. a   5. c

Set 39: Answers & Explanations

A. Synonyms

1. prying
2. colourful
3. malicious
4. rebellion
5. diffident
6. insensible
7. descend
8. strut

B. Fill in the blanks

1. marine
2. entangle
3. insulation – material to prevent loss of heat from the body
4. posture
5. meticulous

C. Antonyms

1. flabbergast- to be surprised greatly
2. servile – to humiliate yourself before somebody
3. punish – the opposite of reward
4. accept – to believe as correct
5. adore – like/love very much
6. hasten – to move quickly
7. shortage – not enough of something
8. garrulous – a very talkative person

D. Missing letters

1. active
2. perfect
3. climbers
4. lower
5. recorded

E. Homophones and homographs

1. brace
2. fire
3. recall
4. fire
5. censor
6. recall
7. brace
8. sensor

Set 40: Answers & Explanations

A. Synonyms

1. wizen — to become dry and wrinkled
2. intricate — very detailed
3. fortitude — acting with great courage
4. corroborate — support
5. shackled — restrained
6. perfidy — the state of being disloyal
7. plod — to walk with heavy steps when tired

B. Fill in the blanks

1. gemstones
2. hardest
3. important
4. unrivalled — with no competitors
5. steadfast — cannot be changed; firm

C. Antonyms

1. sporadic
2. vulnerable
3. buoyant
4. unequal
5. negligent
6. straightened
7. inability

D. Missing words

1. adventurer
2. fought
3. outspoken — direct to the point imprisoned
4. treason — to betray one's country
5. imprisoned -- jailed

E. Odd one out

1. snack — All the words relate to food eaten at set time except snack.
2. falcon — All the creatures are amphibians except falcon which is a bird.
3. ice — All the things are hot things except ice.
4. school — All the others are things within a classroom.
5. grasshopper — All are animals except grasshopper which is an insect.

F: Idioms

1. b
2. d
3. e
4. c
5. a

Set 41: Answers & Explanations

A. Synonyms
1. proficient — well-informed in a certain subject, interest or occupation
2. exuberant — full of energy and excitement
3. expostulate — to express a strong disapproval to something
4. apportion — to share something evenly
5. susceptible — likely to be harmed by a particular thing
6. villain — an evil person; wicked
7. candid — frank, honest
8. vitality — state of being strong and capable

B. Fill in the blanks
1. expensive   2. digested   3. commercial   4. pest   5. protect

C. Antonyms
1. terrestrial — something related to Earth and its residents
2. frivolous — not serious; having little or no importance
3. enthralling — to capture someone's attention
4. gladiatorial — willing to fight, combative
5. improvise — design something without advance planning
6. dexterous — very skilful especially with the use of one's hands
7. triumph — win a famous victory
8. obedience — following the rules

D. Missing letters
1. prey — an animal being hunted to become food   2. character   3. inject
4. unable   5. lure — tempt, attract

E. Homophones and homographs
1. fly   2. row   3. pane   4. attribute
5. pain   6. row   7. fly   8. attribute

Set 42: Answers & Explanations

A. Synonyms

1. cognizant — being aware of
2. impediment — hindrance; a defect in speech
3. contritely — being moved by conscience and guilt; remorseful
4. discord — disagreement; lack of coordination
5. clandestine — to be done secretly
6. surplus — leftovers; an excess in the production of supplies
7. measure — give a calculated answer to a problem

B. Fill in the blanks

1. ecosystem – a biological community of organisms
2. larger
3. visible
4. corals
5. preservation

C. Antonyms

1. constrain
2. desirous
3. withhold
4. embroil
5. abet
6. sloppy
7. mischief

D. Missing words

1. predators
2. torpedo
3. prey
4. pup
5. live

E. Odd one out

1. chalk — All the items are edible except chalk.
2. fresh — All the words describe taste except fresh.
3. horror — All the words are types of dance except horror.
4. Glasgow — All are places are American states except Glasgow.
5. Gandhi — All the leaders are past presidents of the USA except Gandhi.

F: Idioms

1. d
2. a
3. b
4. e
5. c

Printed in Great Britain
by Amazon